Faith
OVER
FEAR

How my mom's fear of breast cancer became my fight

JOANNE AMERUOSO

Cover design by Melissa Williams Design
Front photo painted by Vito Ameruoso Sr.
Editing by Yvette Dano

Foreword

What can I say about this lovely woman? She reached out and opened up to me about her own experiences with breast cancer in her family and her own fight as a previvor, but not before she let me share mine. Asking questions, she showed compassion and listened. And all this because of "the connection." The connection that I didn't know existed. The connection that I desperately needed. The connection that I have gratefully learned that all breast cancer patients have. We all have the unwritten, all-powerful and spiritual connection that only WE truly understand. I've learned from so many amazing warriors. From breast-baring bathroom buddies showing the scars that I know do not compare to the permanently scarred heart and soul, and the emotional turmoil that we all endure. The fear and hopefully the relief. The answers to the immediate questions. The sharing of doctors, support groups, and the do's and the don'ts of how to navigate this new journey that so many of us are faced with. Be kind to yourself, there are no stupid questions and you are your best advocate. In the meantime; and with the help of this book, you will find some of the answers. We are a community and we are WOMEN, so please don't ever forget that you're never alone. Together we are one.

Gioia Bruno

Introduction

As I sit here at the cemetery on Mothers Day, it's been a little over 7 years since my beautiful mother lost her battle to breast cancer. I can't help but to feel compelled to write this book. Not just for the sake of my healing, but to honor some of the most courageous women in my life . . . my grandmother, my mother, my aunts and some amazing friends I have lost to breast cancer. I also know that along this journey of writing, I will grow tremendously. I know that in writing this book it will truly enable me to no longer harbor the anger and despair I felt upon my mother's passing or hold onto the . . . "whys" and "she would still be here with us, if only!" I am sure that I will be flooded with emotions throughout this journey, and will be doing some real deep soul searching along the way, as well as being transparent. No feelings or emotions will be held back. Why do I feel so compelled to tell my story, you may ask? And what makes this so different from anyone else's story? Well, I'll tell you. This book is to show you just how courageous my mother and grandmother were, and how they left an everlasting mark. You will learn how brave someone can be when there is no choice, no matter what they are up against! You will read how determination can defeat the odds. My goal is to let you know that you are never alone, even when you feel that you are. Stay educated, be your own advocate, you are your biggest fan in life. You will be encouraged to fight hard when your back is pushed up against the wall, even when you feel defeated. You DIG deep, real deep to find the strength that you've never known you had. FAITH over FEAR! Stand up not only to cancer, but to anything in life, and when the fear becomes bigger than you, make it your fight! You can look fear in the face and say "NO MORE FEAR!" It's False Evidence Appearing Real. If someone had told me that one day I would be writing a book, I would have said, "You're crazy!" And yet here I am. I hope that along this journey, while reading my story, you can put yourself in my shoes to see just how my mom's fear of breast cancer became my fight!

Chapter 1

Genetics

Everyone has heard the saying, "I got dealt the wrong cards." Usually, this is a feeling some people might have towards the end of their lives, but I began to feel that way at a very young age. I believe I was around eleven years old when I began my menstrual cycle. This was the moment when I morphed from a girl into a young woman. As crazy as it might sound, we were excited to wear this badge of honor. We couldn't wait to tell all our girlfriends "the big news." Except, this milestone was a little different for me. Almost immediately I suffered from painful periods. This became the pattern early on every time my "friend" would come around. I never understood why they referred to this monthly plague as our "friend." I think if you asked any girl, she would rather not call it that. From the first time I got it, there was no normalcy. It always lasted seven to thirteen days, and I suffered a heavy flow, alongside severe cramps (eventually leading me to live off of Anaprox, an anti-inflammatory drug). This was unheard of for someone so young, and it went on for years. I missed countless days of school and other important functions. I was crippled by the cramps. There were days when the pain was so debilitating I couldn't get out of bed.

By the time I was twenty years of age, I knew something wasn't right. Unfortunately, during this time of my life, my days were consumed with helping take care of my boyfriend Dino, my best friend, who had just been diagnosed with testicular cancer. All along, I was completely ignoring the fact that my own symptoms were getting worse. Nothing else mattered, my boyfriend was a priority. I truly loved him. I needed to be by his side every step of the way, even though my own pain was becoming unbearable. A year of putting myself on the backburner to care for Dino passed by, and sadly so did he. To say I was devastated, would be an understatement. He wasn't just my boyfriend. I had lost my best friend of eleven years. A friend who loved me unconditionally, whom I made endless memories with. Never did we let a day go by, without saying I love you. At such a young age, my entire world was rocked. Feeling this incredible loss at the age of twenty one was a life lesson I would never forget. What I took from the bravery and courage that Dino displayed was that no matter what life throws at you . . . you fight.

With nothing but time on my hands now, I realized how much these painful periods had evolved in the past year. My mom and I spoke and decided it was time to focus on me. I needed to get to the bottom of why this was happening. The pain was exhausting me. I spent the next year in and out of doctor's offices, with my mom right by my side. I was scared, worried and the pain was getting worse. Finally, mom and I found a new doctor who had new suspicions. She knew I was dealing with more than painful cramps and was committed to getting to the bottom of the situation. *Finally*, I thought, *someone who was listening to me.* After a brief examination, she seemed to think that I had a disease called endometriosis. *Endo what?* I thought. Oddly, my mom seemed to be familiar with this word. As for me, I couldn't even pronounce it. The doctor tried to briefly explain the disease in layman's terms, but I really had no clue just how debilitating this disease could become until she said the words, "If in fact if this is what I think it is, I have to tell you, you may not be able to have children one day." *Wait, what did she just say?* My head was spinning. The doctor continued to say, "and if you can conceive, it will only be with the help of fertility doctors, it won't be a natural occurrence." I began to cry. "What do you mean, how bad is this?" I asked. I truly had no clue. I had never heard of this disease before, nor could I even pronounce the word. The doctor continued to explain how endometriosis is caused by your body producing too much estrogen, it spreads to the organs and causes scar tissue everywhere it touches. "I suggest that you try to have kids very young, because as you get older this will just get progressively worse," she said. So basically at the age of twenty one, my "biological clock" was ticking. Talk about a punch to the gut! All I ever wanted was a big family, like the one I came from. I wanted to be just like my mom raising a large family. My mother was such an incredible image of what a mother should be. I wanted to follow in her footsteps. (Little did I know just how much I was already following in her footsteps.) When people would ask me what I wanted to do for a living, I would respond, "Duh, be a stay-at-home mom." This honestly was my desire. So having this horrible news thrown at me knocked me down. I didn't even know how to begin to absorb this. *What the hell do we do next?* I thought.

My mother and I had a unique relationship. We did everything together, and I mean everything . . . we cooked, baked, cleaned and shopped together, we cried, we laughed and shared so many special moments. I simply loved her. In her eyes, she was raising me to be the "perfect" Italian daughter. Her dream for me was that I marry and have a family just like hers. She was my best friend, so much so that she stood as my Matron of Honor at my wedding. I came from a household of four older brothers. As the youngest and only girl . . . to say I was special, was an understatement. I was the "gem," as people would say. Daddy's little girl, and mommy's precious gem. My mother had always been there for me in some of the roughest times, especially the past year, while mourning the loss of my boyfriend. I knew I could lean on her once again. I knew that she understood what I was going through. My mom had five children by the time she was only twenty eight years old, and a hysterectomy at the young age of thirty one, though she never told me why. One thing she did tell me was that when she was pregnant with me, she also had a fibroid tumor growing inside the uterus, which was preventing me from getting the nutrients I needed. She used to tease me and tell me that my head was the size of an orange, weighing in at only 5 pounds at birth. After my birth, she continued to have a multitude of problems, which eventually led to her hysterectomy. She never told me what those problems were. I knew that she had some pregnancy struggles leading to miscarriages, yet she never really explained why. At this point, I had to find the facts and what she went through. I was curious to know my family DNA. I had questions that needed answers. *Would I be forced to follow in her genetic footsteps? What did all of this mean?* Considering that my maternal grandmother was a two-time breast cancer survivor and apparently also had endometriosis, it was time to do some digging.

On the car ride home, I was an emotional wreck. My mom tried to keep me calm. "So she's basically saying if I don't think about having kids soon, I may never be able to have children. This is only going to get worse, and time isn't on my side right now," I cried. This was the only thing I cared about in the moment. Having just lost my boyfriend, whom I had planned to marry, I now had no one in my life. Things began to look even worse. "That's not true, look at me," my mother said. "What do you mean, what happened to you?" "Well, I had miscarriages in between your brothers, and the doctors back then knew I had endometriosis. This was what was causing me to lose the babies," my mom said. "Oh my God, Mom, you never told me that," I said, shocked. "Well, one thing they did know was that I was producing too much estrogen, which was basically what caused the endometriosis," she said (*and breast cancer*, I thought to myself). "But I didn't let that stop me." This was the first time I had ever heard this from my mom. I was blown away by what she had just shared with me. "Come on, you have to stay positive," she said. My mother was my voice of reason, even though I couldn't help but wonder why she didn't share all of this with me sooner. I remember her specifically saying to me, "Don't listen to the doctors, they don't always know it all." I will never forget those words. For some reason, my mom was not a big believer in doctors.

Heading home to tell my dad was quite embarrassing. Back then you just didn't speak to your father about "girl stuff". I overheard my mom explaining things to him from the other room. In came my dad, walking into the kitchen where I was, and wrapped his big strong arms around me. My dad always made me feel safe. "It's going to be okay. We are here for you," he said. Knowing that I had my parents, who were so supportive, was helpful. I knew I wasn't alone. They were always my and my brothers biggest supporters.

I decided it was time to begin my research. I wanted to know more about this disease and specifically my family history. It began to dawn on me that the women in my family were screwed genetically. I knew that too much estrogen played a key role in contributing to breast cancer. Now I was curious, more than ever, to know my risks. One thing that I didn't know back then, is that too many people focused on the BRCA gene, a genetic marker that meant you're at higher risk for developing breast cancer, not realizing there were many other mutations that played a role. The more I researched, the more I discovered how important it was to know your family history, as well as your environmental history. Realizing that I needed to become an advocate for myself, I became active in walking the breast cancer walks in honor of my grandmother, a two-time survivor. I volunteered, helping to raise money to be put towards "finding a cure," and did my due diligence to gain as much knowledge as I could. For some reason I felt this was important, even though I had no idea just how much this disease would eventually impact my family.

As focused as I was on breast cancer, I couldn't ignore endometriosis. (It spreads like wildfire, some say, with other doctors comparing its spread to cancer.) I was learning that endometriosis can cause swelling, bleeding and pain, which I had already experienced firsthand. This is because the tissue grows and bleeds in areas where it can't easily get out of the body, developing scar tissue that can web onto other organs, causing major problems like infertility and a heightened risk for cancer. Another problem endometriosis causes is what's known as a "chocolate cyst." This is when an ovarian cyst fills with old menstrual blood, and eventually erupts. These cysts are extremely painful and can interfere with fertility. The more I read, the more educated I became on the severity of the disease. I was learning that my cancer risk was to be taken seriously due to the over abundance of estrogen in my body, and my grandmother having had breast cancer twice. I knew I had to be an advocate for myself and also my mom. I remember thinking, *yes, the genetic cards we were dealt indeed sucked!* But after a lot of good cries and some diligent research, I was determined to beat the odds. I was not going to let any of these factors steal my dream of being a mother one day.

My mom was a worrier, and her way of dealing with things (in her own words) was, "If you tell yourself you're not going to get it, then you won't." Truth be told, she used to say this so much, I almost began to believe it myself. But the difference between me and my mother was that I was determined to be an advocate. I was diligent with my regular check ups, and would argue with her endlessly to do the same. With the genetic factors slapping us right in the face, I knew I had to get my mom onboard to be more proactive for herself. She had never gone for a regular mammogram or breast examination. I knew how important the diagnostics were, but she was not having it. *Was she afraid?* Looking back, I would say yes. She often used the phrase, "If I ever have breast cancer, you will never know. I am not kidding." I remember thinking, *what the hell does she mean by that? Why would she say something so ridiculous?* Having just lost my boyfriend to cancer, this blew my mind. *How could she know the fact that her own mother just battled breast cancer, and yet know the risks?* The importance of "early detection" was well known. I knew I had to get her to be more aware.

I decided to make a mammogram appointment for my mom

without her knowing. I called her up with the excuse of taking her out for lunch. When she got in the car, I told her the plan. Immediately she said, "Pull over, let me out, now," as she began to swing the car door open. I could not believe her reaction to a simple mammography. It broke my heart to see how upset she got with me. I couldn't understand it. "Why are you so afraid?" I asked her. "Wouldn't you want to know early, rather than find out too late?" "No, take me home now," she said. I could tell she was beginning to panic. "Okay, okay, close the door, I won't take you there, I promise!" I saw my mother was actually shaking. She turned to me and with a stern voice said, "I am not joking with you, if I ever have breast cancer, you will never know! And that's because I don't want to know!"

This was so profoundly disturbing to me. It made me sad, yet so angry. *Why was she so fearful? Why wouldn't she want to try everything in her power to avoid this horrible cancer? How would I ever get her to see things differently? Why didn't she have a sense of urgency like I did?* I just couldn't wrap my head around her way of thinking. We had many heated discussions and arguments about cancer prevention on many different occasions, to the point that I would walk out. I tried, I really tried, to make her see the importance of preventative care. I even got on my dad's case about it. I would ask him, "Why are you not pushing her to go?" He would say, "I tried, she's just too scared." I knew one of the biggest reasons she wouldn't get checked was that she was very claustrophobic. The thought of having an MRI made her nervous. There was something within her that was so fearful, and I didn't realize how scared she really was. Yet, as a mother, she showed strength and confidence. But not when it came to being an advocate for herself. One thing I did know was that she witnessed my grandmother go through surgeries and dreadful treatments, that must have been frightening for her and her sister to see. I would have thought that experience would make her want to be more of an advocate.

I was so fearful, I made up my mind and knew that I would do anything to avoid breast cancer. Especially knowing that I had this abundance of estrogen flowing through me. I was the complete opposite of my mother. I was determined to make her realize that if cancer was caught early enough, it can be beat. I tried to lead the way by example, thinking she would follow. I even begged her to go with me. "Let's do it together," I would say. There were times I thought I was making progress and changing her mind, only to find out she was just appeasing me, with no intention of really going for a checkup. Basically, she was saying "yes" just to shut me up. This made me frustrated, and more determined to get her on board.

Chapter 2

My Hero

To say that my grandmother was the life of the party was an understatement. Her laughter and smile lit up a room when she was around. She had a vibrant presence about her. She loved to sing and dance, whenever given the opportunity. Grandma was charismatic, smart, beautiful, caring, silly, loving, funny, and most certainly courageous. Her birth name was Maria, but people called her Mary. There was nothing *not* to love about her. She was truly so loving, and lived to please her family. The happiest of times for her was when she was with her grandchildren, cooking, baking and making sure everyone was happy. We were her pride and joy. Just like my mom, family was everything to her. Coming from a large Italian family herself, she knew the importance of Sundays. This was by far her favorite day. It usually involved homemade pasta, delicious meatballs, and "gravy" as she called it. Every Sunday, without fail, ended with a round of cards ("May I"). Grandma made sure to pass down the recipes; always having us get our hands dirty and teaching us all the techniques. Some of the best memories I have are hand-rolling the pasta, making the ravioli, and oh yes . . . those anisette cookies, with the little colored sprinkles that would make a mess and get everywhere. My grandmother lived for those moments. Family traditions were so important to her. She made every holiday special—from Christmas to Easter, birthdays and backyard barbecues, the endless New Year's Eve parties that were priceless. You name it, she did it. Grandma would make my cousins and me beautiful matching velvet party dresses to wear for the holidays.

Some of my most cherished memories are the endless sleepovers I had with her and Grandpa. Being raised in a household with four boys, I couldn't wait to come home from school on a Friday, pack my bags and go spend the weekend with my grandma. I can still remember sitting on her lap getting the most awesome back scratches and hugs. My favorite thing to do was to lie in bed with her and watch a good movie. We polished our nails, played cards, sang and danced. She really loved to dance with me and be silly. (I definitely know where I got my love of dance.) As a family, we had plenty of road trips to Disney, Florida and the Poconos, while enjoying the Amish traditions and picking some corn. One of her favorite things to do was to eat at the Amish restaurants. The car rides were filled with endless laughs and fun, all of us packed into a station wagon piled on top of each other's laps. Since there were no seatbelt laws, it was a challenge to see how many people we could squeeze in at once. We may not have had all the riches, but we certainly had all the fun, and most importantly we had each other.

Grandma was a woman of many talents. She worked many

jobs throughout her life and had many hobbies. The most enjoyment she had was betting on the horses at Off-Track Betting (OTB), and playing the daily lotto numbers. We used to beg her to let us pick the horses for her. My grandparents definitely had a knack for winning. They got much enjoyment out of this sport. My grandmother didn't need much, it was the little things in life that made her happy. And winning made her happier. It was the best part of betting, because if in fact she won, all the grandkids would get a few bucks each. Sometimes my parents would take my grandparents to Atlantic City for the day. Grandma loved to play the penny slot machines. She always had a great story to tell. Depending on whether she won or lost, would determine her mood the next day. Another of her favorite hobbies was to knit. As a little girl, I used to beg her to make me ponchos. I think I had one in every color (including one pastel rainbow color, which was my favorite). Grandma was incredible and very special to me. I loved her so much. We all did!

Most of my memories of my grandma being sick with breast cancer are vague. I can say I am blessed to have more beautiful memories than unpleasant ones. I was young, yet I remember certain things. I saw my mom cry quite a few times and never understood why. My mom tried to hide a lot from me. My brothers were a little older, so they understood more than I did. There were many times grandma would have to come stay with us because she was ill. I was probably about four or five years old, and grandma was about fifty eight years old when she had her first battle with breast cancer. I was so young, I really had no clue what was happening around me. I do recollect going to visit her in the hospital. We weren't allowed to actually go into the room. My brothers, cousins and I brought her gifts. We waved to her through the glass window. I saw her, an angel in a blue gown.

I couldn't fathom what was happening. How could I understand how brave she was when I didn't understand the situation? As I got older, I learned that she had what is called a partial mastectomy, which is the removal of one breast. Apparently this was just the beginning of her cancer experience. Grandma was facing six weeks of radiation treatments, five days a week. My mother was a stay-at-home mom, and her sister worked full-time. So together, they would take care of my grandmother. There were times she would have to stay with us, due to the fact that she needed constant care. I learned later in life that she went to hell and back. Back in the 70's, they didn't have drugs to combat the side effects of radiation or to lessen the severity of the side effects; one pretty much suffered through it without a choice. It was torture. The radiation left her with burns and scars. Years later, she developed lymphoedema in her arm, causing her more pain and suffering. This was so damaging my grandmother decided she would never put herself through that pain and anguish again. What she did do was put up a good fight. She was the epitome of the definition of a warrior. This woman had so much determination, she was not one to give up.

I believe this not only scarred my grandmother, but it also frightened my mother. It would only make sense. When you witness someone you love tremendously endure this type of pain, it hurts and leaves an impression that cannot be erased. My mom, my aunt and the rest of the family gave my grandmother so much love and support. They had to take care of her in ways I'm sure they never imagined. I learned this was when my family came together and fought together. I can tell you, for sure, that my mom and her sister were the strength that held my grandmother together. She knew she was never alone in her fight. She was lucky to have such amazing and caring daughters. As I got older my mom made sure to tell me how Grandma never let cancer take her down. She fought gracefully and always had a smile. The one thing I do remember was my grandmother always smiling. My mother used to say, "I don't think I could ever endure what she has been through." This is where my mom's fear began. *Should I have known?* Always conscious that breast cancer could be passed down genetically, I'm sure it wasn't ever far from my mother's mind.

Time passed and Grandma healed. My mom and my aunt were diligent with her continued care. They made sure she stayed on top of her check-ups, hoping that she had beaten the disease. Unfortunately, breast cancer had its own agenda, and it didn't waste much time. Two years later, it returned to the other breast. This cancer was aggressive. Once again, my beautiful, courageous grandmother had another battle to fight, facing yet another partial mastectomy. The one thing that was different this time was that my grandmother was *not* having it. She was determined to kick the "shit" out of cancer, but Grandma was going to do it her way or no way at all. This meant no treatments. I was so young, about seven or eight years old, I didn't completely understand what was going on. I could only imagine how my mom and my aunt felt at the time. Why would my grandmother choose this route, when doctors always instill so much hope with these treatments? You always want someone to fight for the best possible outcome. But while Grandma's choice was unheard of and unconventional, it was her choice. I may have been young, but I do remember her determination. She was a fighter. She wasn't going to let anything stand in the way of her life choices. Grandma said, "no more." No more radiation, and no more burns. For the people who loved her, I am sure this decision was difficult to accept, especially for my mom and aunt.

But no one could judge my grandmother for her choice, having never walked in her shoes.

Surgery came and went, and Grandma decided to take a more holistic route. Finding a nutritionist, she began a regimen of vitamins. Quite honestly, she never cared about what people thought. Keep in mind, reconstructive surgery wasn't what it is today. Not too many women took the route of breast reconstruction. As for Grandma, she decided to "stay flat", "So what?" she would say. It wasn't going to change or define the person she was. She took it all in stride. I can remember plenty of times going for bra fittings with her and my mom. My mom and I would wait in the fitting room and then here she'd come, trying on different size "boobies" as she would call them. She would make us laugh so hard as she modeled asking, "How do these boobies look on me?" She was just so lighthearted and silly about it. There were endless jokes about her fake boobies. In fact, one of her first mastectomy bras had silicone that you would insert into the bra, allowing you to choose your size. Grandma was so light-spirited about them. She would joke all the time. Once when my cousin and I were getting into trouble at a family gathering, by interrupting the "adult's card game," Grandma whipped out one of her silicone implants and said, "Here, go play Hot Potato with this!" I can actually still see her smiling and laughing as she did it. On another occasion my grandparents were staying with us for the weekend. Whenever they slept over, they would sleep upstairs in my brother's room. One morning, like so many others, Grandma came downstairs. I looked at her and said, "Grandma, you forgot to put your boobs on, go back up and put them on." She looked at me with her devilish smile and said, "I don't feel like wearing them today." "Grandma!" I laughed. And there was my grandfather chuckling "Come on Mary, go back up and put them on." Of course, he didn't care if she wore them. He loved her to pieces. The two of them were just so funny together, like a comedy act. Do you think he really cared if she wore them or not? No way, they had a special relationship. She was not going to let body image define who she was. My mom used to say to me, "I don't know who you take after." Well, I knew . . . my grandmother. Unlike me, my mom was a little more reserved and on the shy side. I was silly like my grandmother. Instead of going back up to get her own boobs, she would say to me, "run upstairs and go get my boobies for me, Joannie" with that silly grin on her face. By the way, that's what she called me all the time, Joannie. And you bet I did. I would come marching down the stairs with her bra on over my shirt, chanting . . . "boobies, boobies, take a look at these!" She would find this so hysterical! There I was in the kitchen dancing around in her prosthesis bra, (which by the way, no longer had silicone inserts, they were now padded to size). She was so cute, my grandmother. She had twig legs, and a little Italian pot belly. My dad used to tease her and say, "Be careful of what you eat, or you may have to size up that bra one day!" She didn't care what anyone said. She was beyond lighthearted about this, and would just laugh! This was a woman with so much determination to live life to the fullest, she would not let anything get in her way. She always displayed to her family that fear wasn't an option in her world. These were just some of the priceless memories that keep me laughing to this day. To know my grandmother was to love her.

Chapter 3

A Closer Look

By the age of twenty one, I was living in misery every month. I decided I had put my health on the back burner long enough. There were so many times I missed doing things with my family. My mother always felt bad about leaving me behind, while lying on the couch with heating pads across my stomach, and basically feeling like crap. She would make up excuses for me (because I tended to be very private about this) when I couldn't go to gatherings. After doing countless scans, there was only so much the doctors could see. Surgery seemed to be unavoidable at this point, but I was averting it having never had an operation before. I was scared, especially after seeing all that my boyfriend had gone through. I told myself that compared to his suffering, surgery was nothing. For once in my life, I had no choice but to put the fear out of my head and do what I had to do. The surgery date was set, it was decided that my dad would take me to the hospital on the big day. Considering my mom's fear of hospitals and insistence at avoiding them at all costs. Her anxiety would have made mine worse anyway. My dad, on the other hand, was the calm one. Always the voice of reason. And then we had Fran, my mom's best friend, who lived across the street from us. Not only was she family and considered me a daughter, she worked as a nurse at the hospital where the surgery was scheduled. She knew I was nervous about the anesthesia because I was asthmatic, so she kept reassuring me that everything would be fine. It put me at ease knowing she would be there.

It was a big day for me, I would finally get some real answers. Driving to the hospital, my dad was cracking jokes trying to distract me, of course. The surgery was scheduled for early afternoon. I had the entire morning to sit around and make myself nervous. My dad could clearly see how scared I was. I don't know what I was more nervous about, what the doctors would find or whether or not I would wake up. Holding my hand as we walked into the hospital, I remember him squeezing it, as if to say . . . *I got you!* My dad wasn't a mushy kind of guy, but he had his way of letting me know that he loved me. Arriving at the hospital, I was checked in and ready to go. The nurses asked my dad to step out, while they prepped me. By the time he came back, I was a basket case. He kept making the nurses laugh with his sarcasm, but I wasn't finding it funny. I knew what he was doing, but I was too nervous. Nothing could distract me. Fran stopped by to check in on me. By the time the anesthesiologist walked in, I was clenching my inhaler in my hand. I must have asked him ten times to please make sure my inhaler was with me when I woke up. My biggest fear was that I would have an asthma attack while in surgery. The doctor laughed and said, "I'm going to give you something to calm you right now, then when we get in the O.R. I'll knock you out right away!" He must have seen the panic in me. I failed to see the humor. But after he gave me a little sedation, got me on the stretcher and wheeled me into the elevator, I was feeling good. Apparently, so good that I looked up at the anesthesiologist and said with a raised fist, "I'll give ya knock you out!" My dad thought this was hysterical, and told this story for weeks after my surgery. I guess they both had a good laugh on my account. Then the doctor told me to give my dad a kiss goodbye as it was time to go to the O.R. Drugged up as I was, I started crying. My father was just amazing. As he wiped my tears he said to me, "Come on sweetheart, it's going to be okay. It will be over before you know it." Wheeling me into the O.R., I remember thinking, *man it's so cold in here*. The next thing I recall, while lying on the table, was seeing this big white light over me and a voice saying, "count back from 100 and take a deep breath . . ."

"Joanne, Joanne," is what I heard next. I thought I was dreaming. *What? It's over already?* As I opened my eyes I saw a familiar face, and Fran telling me to wake up that everything was fine. I remember all I wanted to do was sleep. Who wanted to wake up? Ironically, this was the best nap I had ever had. In recovery, I got to see my dad. He was so happy, holding my hand and telling me, "See, I told you it would be over quickly." I didn't know from long or short. I had no conception of time. I felt like I was sleeping for hours! As I became more alert, I was anxious to get home and into my own bed. What I really wanted to do was see my mom. I finally got the okay to go home. It seemed like we waited forever. It was late evening as I walked through the door into my home. You could see the sense of relief on my mother's face. She had everything prepared for me and got me all propped up in bed. Then came my big question, "what did the doctors see?" Their educated guess was right. I did indeed have endometriosis. "The doctor said it was pretty bad, and that it was in a few different spots," she said. "They cleaned it out the best they could." From all the research I'd done, I knew this meant I was screwed. This was a temporary fix, a Band-Aid so to speak. Of course, at this moment I was thinking *will I ever be able to have children?* This was a real concern for me. Little did I know that this would be the first of many surgeries to come. I had no control over this disease that had been running havoc through my body.

Other than being emotionally upset, I was actually feeling pretty good the first couple of hours that I was home. Suddenly, the pain began to set in. The medications were subsiding, and then came the unexpected. The pain radiated throughout my entire upper body, from my fingertips to my stomach. I started to panic, begging my parents to take me back to the hospital. I thought something was wrong. By this time Fran was home from work, so my mom called her and asked her to come over. And of course she did. She was always there for us. (That's why we nicknamed her Nurse Fran.) She explained that this was normal pain from the gasses that were inserted into the belly to expand and look around. She definitely calmed me down, and explained that I needed to move around a little to get the gas moving. With this reassurance, I was able to stay calm and tough it out through the night. With each day that passed, even with the grim news hanging over my head, I slowly got better and tried to stay positive. At my post-op visit with the doctor, we had a lengthy discussion. They were up front and honest with me, but I already knew my reality. They didn't have to tell me. I had done my homework on this disease, and I knew my chances were slim to none when it came to conceiving, at least on my own. My grandmother, my boyfriend, and of course my mom taught me at a young age to never lose faith. My mom beat the odds of endometriosis and had five children, so why couldn't I? She was living proof that I could overcome this disease. At the young age of twenty one, my biological clock was ticking. This didn't happen to most women until they were middle-aged. It was something I couldn't wrap my head around. I had to have faith, there was no other option.

Trusting that I was in good hands, I had the doctors keep a close eye on me and held on to the hope I learned to have at a young age. I had lost the person I planned to marry and build a family with. The words faith and hope became so prevalent in my life at that time. I held on to so much hope for my boyfriend, always encouraging him to never lose his faith. Together we learned that without it, we had nothing. We both became closer to God than I ever thought we would. We constantly clung on to what we always believed as Christians, that God is good and miracles do happen. With God by our side, we always tried to find the positive in the negative. Faced with adult-like issues, I grew up awfully fast at twenty one. Finding myself alone, I was struggling to keep my own faith. It had been easier to encourage Dino than it was to keep myself optimistic. I was still mourning the loss of my beloved Dino and of potentially having children. It truly was difficult to stay positive. What a familiar thing the loss of time was to me. *Why do we constantly try to calculate time when that window seems so small?* Things again were looking so bleak. There were many nights I cried, afraid of the unknown future that I was facing. What a whirlwind of emotions this year had brought me. And my mother was there for me every step of the way. I don't know how I would have gotten through these difficult times in my life without her.

Chapter 4

Life As I Knew It

With the passage of time, some things got better . . . and some things got worse. Two years later, I met someone and got engaged. I was constantly in and out of doctor's offices, battling the disease. The dreaded "chocolate cysts" were causing my periods to worsen. One grew so big it ruptured, causing the most excruciating pain. The only way I can describe it is an electrifying pain crawling all the way through my body, from my shoulders down to my legs. The doctors had no choice but to go in and perform an emergency D&C. They needed to "clean me out" and stay on top of things so it wouldn't worsen. Not only were these cysts painful, but they were life-threatening as well. (Internal bleeding can be dangerous!) This was the first of many more D&C's for me. I had to keep myself positive, yet always aware of what the doctors told me so early on, that childbirth more than likely wasn't in my future. I was never the type of person to just sit back and let things happen. I learned at an early age, that you look for a way to maneuver and beat the odds. I knew time was slipping away from me, but I was determined not to let this disease dictate my life. Still, in many aspects it did. I spent many days crippled by the pain, and there were plenty of emotional days that consumed me. My mother was the only one who could really understand what I was going through having battled the same disease. She was always there for me, and knew what I needed to get through my days. I never imagined the path that was before me, but the worse this endometriosis got the more determined I became.

I planned my wedding around my menstrual cycle. I knew that if I didn't my period would just completely ruin my wedding day. It was 1993 and I was now married. With the obvious issue of a ridiculous timeline, we decided to begin to try and conceive. The endometriosis was getting progressively worse. Having had a recent D&C, to once again "clean me out," we didn't waste any time. I needed to find the right doctor, because I was tired of hearing the words, "Well you know, without fertility drugs you will never be able to conceive." I wasn't going to settle until I heard what I wanted to hear from a doctor. I wanted someone who was going to see the hopeful side of things. I didn't want to depend on medicine to give me children . . . I wanted to depend on God! For some reason, I was dead set against fertility drugs or in vitro. I wanted to exhaust natural options before I took that route. I always had it in my head that I could beat the odds. Finally, I found a doctor who believed I had a chance at conceiving on my own. Someone who said the words I wanted to hear, and he specialized in this disease. I loved how compassionate he was, and how he told me from day one to never give up. He gave me hope by telling me that often when women get pregnant, the endometriosis can sometimes in fact get better. He agreed that time was of the essence, and also believed I had a chance of conceiving naturally. A slim chance at best. That was really all I ever wanted to hear, it gave me a glimmer of hope. Walking out of his office, that's exactly what I had newfound hope and a much better perspective on things. Feeling more confident now than I had in a long time, I kept in mind that this pregnancy was indeed possible. With no time to waste, I continued to see this particular doctor, and together we made a plan of action.

Throughout the years, I'd been put on birth control pills to lessen the severity of my periods, because the bleeding was getting worse. Eventually, the doctor took me off the pills. Although I was still dead set against fertility drugs, he somehow convinced me to try fertility hormone shots. Against my better judgment, I made the appointments for the regime of shots and agreed to go ahead with the plan. I was not happy about this at all. As a matter of fact, I was angry! Not only did I have to frequently go to be monitored, but the shots were painful and annoying. I also began to pack on weight. Weeks of this nonsense went on and on, and nothing was helping me. In fact, I felt worse. Until one day I finally said, "enough!" I knew from the start, this was not what I wanted. Feeling defeated and frustrated, I was ready to throw in the towel. Enough was enough. I needed to re-evaluate how badly I wanted a baby. Mentally I was drained. I needed to step back and take a break from all of this. I needed time to sort through my priorities and really think things through. My body was so hormonally confused. I decided to stop everything. By everything, I meant even focusing on trying. I was becoming consumed with pregnancy and it was extremely stressful. I would have stood on my head if someone told me that would work! And that was exactly why I didn't want to start any sort of infertility drugs to begin with. I made up my mind, and held on to the belief that if I was going to have a child it was going to happen naturally. With this new mindset, I continued on with life and put pregnancy on the back burner. I decided to leave this up to God. I told myself, if it's meant to be then it will be.

Suddenly a twist. Things began to shift in my body. Now my menstrual cycle seemed to be going in reverse. I went from having painful periods for years to having no periods at all! The doctors were completely baffled. They began giving me a drug to actually help me produce a period. Imagine, from one extreme to the other! *How can this even happen?* I wanted answers! Thank God I had my mom by my side, without her I would probably have given up. My mom continued to stay positive for me. I continued to pray and leave it up to God. My grandmother, of course, was always beyond encouraging, constantly reminding me that if God wanted me to have a baby, then I would. Those were her words to me. To tell you the truth, I was beginning to lose my faith. I had always been a faithful person, but this was truly testing my ability to believe and stay positive. Sometimes you just sit back and say, *how much more? Is it worth the pain? Will it be worth it in the end?* The unknown was too frightening, and all these obstacles that were in the way seemed to be getting harder to leap over. Now that I was no longer producing a period, I was forced to sit idle and wait to see what was in store for me.

Unfortunately, at this time my beautiful grandmother suffered a stroke. I remember thinking, *what else is God going to throw her way?* It was grave enough that she had to learn how to speak and walk again. I was so scared, I knew I couldn't lose her, we all couldn't. I should have known that this woman, my warrior, my hero of a grandmother, who seemed to be made of steel was not going to let this stroke control her. No way! She was such a staple in our lives. Grandma was a fighter, and once again she was going to fight for her life. Always an example of a pillar of strength, Grandma never let anything stop her. She was covered in a shell of armor. Knowing that she needed to completely heal, my grandmother was determined to battle. It was in her nature to overcome all obstacles. Independence was vital for my grandma and grandpa. It was important for her to learn to drive again, because Grandpa was legally blind. It wasn't easy, and she knew she had leaps and bounds to conquer. That's exactly what she did. In fact, on top of having had a stroke, one night while she was in the hospital (which wasn't giving her the proper care) and not of sound mind, she tried to get out of bed on her own. Grandma ended up falling and breaking her wrist. Yet another hurdle to leap over. In my eyes, it seemed that nothing could ever stop her, truly a fighter. With time, Grandma (with the help of rehab) fully recovered, going back to her somewhat normal life.

At this time in my life, I was working as a nanny on the North shore of Long Island. I was caring for a beautiful family with three children. The parents were both doctors, and worked long hours. This was truly what I loved to do, it made me happy. I always loved working with children. This job definitely kept my mind occupied and busy, which was a good thing for me. Time was passing and I still was not menstruating. My doctor seemed to be mystified as to why this was happening. The doctor I worked for was aware of my situation, and we'd become like family. I confided in her. She was always a voice of reason when I was frustrated with things. After relentlessly trying to conceive, with endless disappointments and all that was going on, I decided to take a much needed vacation away from all of the nonsense. I wanted to have some fun. What better place to have fun than Disney! So I booked it. All I wanted to do was escape and not think about anything. People kept saying to me, when you don't try, that's when you'll get pregnant! Truth or myth, I don't know. But what the hell, I figured I'd give it a try. Besides, this was getting exhausting. I knew one thing for sure, I couldn't keep this up much longer.

March was here, it was my birthday month and a few weeks before the vacation. With the trip so close, suddenly I had come down with strep throat and became very sick. Besides having strep, I was also vomiting a lot. Assuming this was a side effect of the strong antibiotic I didn't question it. The vomiting continued for days. At one point I actually asked myself, *Could I possibly be pregnant*? *Nah, how could that be?* Like I mentioned, I had not had a period in months. A couple of weeks passed and my throat was better, but the vomiting continued, in fact it was worse. I had no clue what could possibly be happening to me. I tried to carry on with my normal routine, but I was also very fatigued. One particular day, after a 45 minute nauseating car ride to work, I made my grand entrance (which was starting to become the norm) by running through the door and going straight to the bathroom. The vomiting was absolutely relentless. There were days I would have to pull over on the parkway, it was like clockwork.

This one particular day, as my normal puking routine ended, I walked out of the bathroom, looked at the doctor I worked for and said "What the hell could this be?" "Well," she said, "I think you should probably consider taking a pregnancy test. I think you may be pregnant." You know the expression *"Do I look like I have 10 heads?"* that's probably the look I gave her at that moment. "No way, how could I possibly be pregnant? I haven't had a cycle in at least six months!" I said. "I think you are," she said with a smile. "Go grab an over-the-counter test today and take it." "Okay, but I really doubt it," I said. (Imagine, doubting a doctor.) Feeling very hesitant about the test, I reluctantly went to the store. *Let me see,* I figured. *I have nothing to lose, right?* I returned to the house. I was so nervous about doing the test. I just didn't want the disappointment anymore. *Here goes nothing,* I thought. I remember laying the test down on the vanity counter, walking into the kitchen, and just pacing back and forth. I was petrified to go back in and see that negative result staring at me once again. Nervous as all hell, I reluctantly walked in, peeked at the stick, almost trying to not look . . . and there it was . . . POSITIVE!! I could not believe my eyes, I truly didn't believe what I was seeing. Grabbing the stick, holding it in disbelief I was crying tears of joy. *Oh my God, can this be for real?* I immediately called my boss at work to tell her she was right. She then suggested that I make an appointment with the OB-GYN right away, which I did. I called my husband, who was of course beyond excited. Then I called my mom. "Mom, you are not going to believe this," I cried. "What?" She immediately thought something was wrong. "I'm pregnant!" I screamed. "What do you mean, how can that be?" My mother was as confused as I was. "I don't know! But I took a test, because of all the throwing up I've been constantly doing, and it's positive!" My mom was now crying with me. "I don't want to tell anyone just yet. I have to make an appointment with the doctor first to make sure this test is right," I warned. She was just bursting at the seams for me. I could hear my grandma in the background asking what was going on, they were so overjoyed! "Okay, but call your father and at least tell him." she said. I hung up with her and immediately called my dad. I can still hear his over-the-moon laugh. He was thrilled for me. His baby was having a baby! Then I immediately called the doctor's office, and they squeezed me in for that night.

Sitting in the office, I almost felt like it was a dream! (And I was also thinking . . . *oh no we just booked a trip to Disney!*) No crazy rides for me, but I didn't care about that. If this was in fact true, this would be the best news ever. The nurse came out to the waiting area and walked me to the back, where she handed me a cup for the urine sample. Once I filled the cup, she said to me, "Go wait in the doctor's office, he'll be right in once we have the results. I kept thinking, *please God let this be true, please!* I was so nervous sitting there, my hands were sweating and my legs were shaking. In walked the doctor, who had been with me during this entire journey. He had a great big smile on his face. Then I heard the words, "Congratulations Joanne, you are pregnant!" I can't even begin to tell you the emotions that went through my body. My eyes were filled, and suddenly there was this sense of relief. It was like hitting the lotto, but certainly much bigger than that. *What is better than the gift of life?* Absolutely nothing! This was what I prayed for from the day I found out that I had endometriosis. "You did it," he said, "you beat the odds, I know how much you wanted this. Come with me, we're going to do a sonogram just to check and see how far you are, and we will run some blood work as well." This was important because I really had no clue when I conceived. Still in disbelief, we shuffled off into the room to do the sonogram, and there it was, this little tiny peanut looking image. It was just surreal. This truly was a miracle. I couldn't believe what I was looking at. I was beyond excited! For the first time, it was real! The tears were streaming down my cheeks. "Well," he said, "not only are you pregnant, but you are about nine weeks pregnant."

"Wait, what? Nine weeks? How could I have not known this?" I asked. "We will run some blood work to be more accurate, but yes, I think about nine weeks." This was by far one of the most incredible days of my life. *Thank you God*, was all I kept saying! God was good to me, giving me my little miracle baby that I had prayed for. And Grandma was right, "If God wants you to have a baby, then you will!" I just couldn't stop smiling (well, and throwing up). Happy Birthday to me! There would never be a better birthday than what I had just received! The gift of life. I was actually going to be a mom. I guess the words faith and hope weren't so overrated after all. Without those words I had nothing. I was completely overjoyed. I could not wait to tell the rest of my family, and I couldn't wait to see my grandmother. I just knew that she would be over the moon for me! I can still see her beautiful smile when she hugged me. She was so excited. The first thing she said was that she couldn't wait to start knitting baby outfits and blankets! Then she said it again, "See Joannie, what did I tell you, I told you, never lose faith." Coming from a two-time breast cancer survivor, and a stroke survivor it was profound for me. That word faith seemed to be such a strong word in my life. I was learning this slowly. And who better to learn it from than my grandmother? Grandma and my mom, more than anyone else, knew how important this was to me.

With my head in the clouds with excitement, I tried to enjoy these moments, but it wasn't easy. The pregnancy seemed to be pretty normal, other than the fact that for nine straight months I was constantly vomiting. So much so, I couldn't even get a prenatal vitamin down my throat. During the entire pregnancy, I threw up so much I only put on sixteen pounds. And the heartburn was just relentless. My mom kept saying, "Oh this baby must have a lot of hair, that's why you have a lot of heartburn!"

I would laugh. Whether this was an Italian myth, or had some truth to it, I guess we were going to find out. Even as I was being wheeled into my birthing room, I was still puking. *I guess this was going to end the same way it started*, I thought to myself.

Overall, it was a rough pregnancy and there were days I felt like I couldn't move. I decided to work until the very end, so there was no choice but to keep going. My due date was on November 7th. But of course, pregnancies don't always end in a timely manner, and I found myself a week overdue. I was just miserable at this point. Grandma was busy, having knitted lots of blankets and outfits for the baby, expecting it to be chilly with winter approaching. November 15th arrived and the labor pains finally hit. The doctors kept sending me home saying I wasn't dilated enough, to go home and walk. On the 17th, I woke up and felt like I was leaking fluid. I knew that my water had not completely broken, but I also knew something wasn't right. Arriving for the third time at the hospital, after having contractions for days now, I looked at my doctor and said, "I am not leaving here without a baby!" He just chuckled. I was also correct, the fluid was leaking and now it was time to break the rest of the membrane. They prepped me and started to give me drugs to accelerate the contractions and dilation. When the doctor went in to break my water, they realized that pretty much all of the fluid had leaked out. Panic set in, now we had no choice but to get the baby out. The baby's heartbeat became extremely low, and there was no time to waste! Only six centimeters dilated, the nurses began to prep the O.R. for a C-section. But I wasn't having it that way, I began to push! The nurse frantically kept saying, "Don't push, you're not ready yet!" *Don't tell me*, I thought . . . *I'm pushing!* This had been one hell of a journey, I was doing it my way now. Finally, after all the struggles, hurdles and disappointments one of the most exciting moments of my life was about to happen. November 17th, 5:15 p.m., my little miracle baby was born. It was a beautiful baby boy we named Rocco. I was in absolute awe. Looking at this beautiful creature that I had created . . . thinking, *I did it*! *I beat the odds!* The chances of conceiving a baby without fertility drugs were almost impossible and with the help of God, I did it. When I held my son in my arms for the first time, I couldn't explain the feeling, he took my breath away. The emotions I felt were just overwhelming. He was so beautiful to me! I immediately fell in love with this little human. Every time I held him in my arms, I kept thinking . . . *I'm finally a mother!* All I wanted to do was hold him and love him, endlessly. I was ecstatic and so was everyone in my family, especially my mom, dad and grandma who shared my struggles with me. Here he was, all 6 pounds, 12oz and a head full of black hair. I guess that Italian myth was right! Rocco had a lot of hair. All of his grandparents couldn't wait to get their hands on him. My mom's first words when she saw him were, "He looks like a Rocco." Not only was his hair jet black, it was spikey! He had the cutest little nose. And the thing that made me even happier was that my warrior grandmother was here to enjoy this moment. It was priceless! Now that we had Rocco, Grandma and Grandpa loved to come and spend time at my mom's more than ever. They enjoyed helping with Rocco every chance they could. They especially enjoyed taking him for walks in the coach carriage that my parents bought for me as a gift. He was like a little prince. Looking for any excuse to take him for a walk, my grandparents enjoyed every second they could. These moments were priceless and life was finally good. God was good!

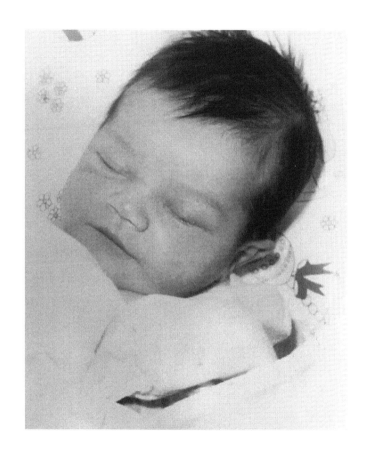

Chapter 5

Moving On

Having this beautiful little boy was a blessing. But, another aspect of life was getting worse. The endometriosis was proving to be relentless. It was around 1997, I was once again trying to get pregnant. Surgeries seemed to be the norm for me. Constantly undergoing D&Cs was the only thing that would help me conceive. I wanted more than anything to give my son a brother or sister. I knew this wasn't going to be easy, but I was determined to beat the odds. Having had an early onset miscarriage already, I was constantly on edge. Not knowing where the road was going to lead me, it was a never-ending roller coaster of emotions. My doctor was always encouraging me to stay positive and not give up. I kept reminding myself, if the doctor had hope, why shouldn't I?

Time went by and I was pregnant once again. This news was joyous, yet frightening at the same time. Of course everyone was excited, especially my mom and grandmother. They all tried to make me see the positive side of things, which was of course was that I was able to conceive on my own. It was the glimmer of hope that I always held onto. I especially remembered the words the doctors had uttered so early on, years ago . . . that I may never be able to have children. This news was a ray of light for me. I wanted to embrace the pregnancy, but I was reluctant knowing the chances of a miscarriage were high. Yet, I set my mind on staying positive, not letting go of hope with this one.

A few months had passed, and the pregnancy seemed to be going just fine. Of course, a "normal" pregnancy for me included constant morning sickness. Although, they called it "morning sickness" it was an all day thing for me. It was a daily struggle, all day, everyday. The one obsession I had that would help settle my stomach was drinking Pepsi Cola with crushed ice. I can still hear my mom saying, "You're going to destroy your teeth by chewing on all that crushed ice!" I was obsessed. I didn't care if I couldn't keep food down, I just needed the damn Pepsi! At this point in my life I also decided to open my own business. I always had a dream of owning a dance studio. After working as a nanny for many years, I decided to follow this dream. Not only follow it, but make it come true. It was extremely difficult to quit my job as a nanny, but I was always up for a new adventure. I've always been about change. In fact I thrived on change! So, I decided to pursue this business, and it turned out to be very successful. I absolutely had my hands full, but I was loving this new experience. Of course, it was extremely difficult when I was in the middle of teaching dance and had to run to the bathroom, because I couldn't hold anything down. I was the type of person who would go do her thing, and then come back and continue as if nothing ever happened. Sounds crazy, but I made it work. The business was thriving and convenient at the same time. I worked late afternoon and nights, so I was able to be home with my son Rocco during the day. This was the perfect scenario for me, and my mom would help me out if I needed it. I was feeling blessed!

Rocco at this point was excited that he was going to have a new baby brother or sister, and I was so over the moon to be able to give him a sibling. Things seemed to be going pretty well until the day I saw some blood. I immediately knew that something wasn't right, this was never a good sign. I quickly called my doctor and they had me go to the office right away. I remember the dreaded phone call I had to make to my Mom. "Mom, you have to take Rocco for me. Something isn't right," I said. "What do you mean?" she asked. "I'm bleeding, I have to go immediately to the doctor," I said. Not knowing what the hell was happening, I grabbed my son, packed up some things for him, and I rushed over to my mom's house. "Will you be okay? Should I come with you?" she asked. My husband was at work and I didn't have time to wait for anyone. She didn't want me to go alone. "No, I'll be okay. You stay with Rocco," I said. I was a complete mess to be honest, but I didn't want her to see me upset. I cried the entire car ride. I knew this wasn't good. Arriving at the office, the doctor was waiting for me. He immediately did the sonogram. He placed the warm gel on my stomach and began to look. He asked me a lot of questions. I had a gut feeling, I knew what he would say next. I saw the look on his face and it wasn't a good one. I was lying there not wanting to ask any questions, because I already knew the answers. He kept looking and looking. I could tell by his expression what was coming. "Please tell me it's okay," I said as I held back the tears. "Joanne, I am so sorry, but I don't hear a heartbeat." "I'm so sorry," the doctor repeated. It was like someone had sucker punched me in the gut. I immediately felt my stomach doing flips. I was devastated. *Why? Why does this have to be so difficult? I thought. Everything always seemed to be an uphill battle. Where do I even go from here?* Have you ever been told the words, "I can't hear the heartbeat"? It's a dagger that stabs you without warning. Lying there, I heard him say the words, "Please don't give up on this." My doctor truly was one of my biggest fans. I could not have asked for a more compassionate medical professional. "This doesn't mean that you won't be able to conceive again, you have to stay positive, look how far you've come." *Did I even want to hear those words? I wasn't even thinking about that yet. This was getting to be too exhausting. All I could think was, what now?* But I knew the answer. Here we go again, yet another hospital visit. The doctor set up the appointment for my D&C. The worst part was waiting for the procedure to be done. The anxiety and anticipation was messing with me. Especially that my body was still reacting as if it was pregnant. I guess hormonally my body was as confused as my frame of mind. I had to walk around looking pregnant, feeling pregnant, knowing my baby was no longer alive inside me.

Now I had to share this unimaginable news with my husband and my family. The first person I wanted to speak to was my dad. So I called the shop where he worked with my brothers. The phone rang, and it was my brother. "Hello," he said, and I was crying. "Hello, are you there?" He could hear me. "It's me," I cried. "What's wrong, Joanne?" he asked. "I lost the baby, I lost the baby," I didn't know what else to say. "What do you mean?" he asked. "I'm miscarrying. I am so sick over this, I just can't do this anymore!" "Okay, just calm down. Where are you? Are you alone?" my brother asked. "Yes, I just left the doctor's office, and I just want to speak to Daddy, please." He handed the phone over to my dad. "Daddy" I cried. "What's the matter, sweetheart?" he asked. (He always called me sweetheart.) I was sobbing at this point. "I lost the baby, I can't believe this is happening," I said. My poor dad had no words, he just listened to me cry. I am certain that he couldn't speak because he himself was crying. "Listen, take a deep breath. It's going to be okay. This is God's way of saying it wasn't meant to be. You have to be strong," he said. I can remember this conversation like it was yesterday. "I don't want to be strong anymore, I am tired of all of this." "Go to Mom's and I'll come home soon," my dad said. Barely able to drive because my eyes were flooded with tears, I headed over to my mom's. I walked in, apparently my dad had called her to tell her the news and she was waiting for me. We didn't say a word, she just wrapped her arms around me and we cried together. Obviously being so young, Rocco had no clue what was happening. He wrapped his arms around my leg to hug me. I picked him up and held him so close and cried. He kept looking at me and hugging me. In his little sweet tiny voice, I heard him say, "You okay mommy?" I kept reminding myself how special he was, and how blessed I was to have him. He was such a sweet soul and always made me smile. I knew it was going to be okay. I still had this beautiful boy to call my son. By now my dad had rushed home, and mom had prepared some lunch for us. I couldn't even think about eating. Once I calmed down a little, I was able to explain everything to my parents. They were so upset for me. Having been through this herself, my mom knew the mental pain and anguish. "I'm going to need your help with Rocco the next few days," I said. I knew it would not be an issue. I could always depend on my mom. I explained that the doctor would call me with the date of the D&C, and that I would be laid up for a few days afterwards. "No problem, just pack some things and bring Rocky here." she said. The night went by, and I left it up to my mom to tell my family. It was just too difficult for me. Once my grandmother heard the news she immediately called me. She never looked at the negative side of things, she had only positive things to say to me. I can honestly say she was the one person who taught me to always take the negative and flip it into a positive. She was always my inspiration because of the love and attitude she displayed. She understood me, having had a miscarriage herself. I slowly began to realize just how strange this was that my mother, my grandmother, and I all had this in common.

A few days had passed and the surgery was booked. I couldn't wait to get the procedure done. I arrived at the hospital and I remember being so weak from the hemorrhage. As soon as I walked in, they sat me in a wheelchair and brought me to the pre-op room. The nurses immediately began to prep me. I sarcastically said to one nurse, "I should have my own personalized cap with my name on it, because I'm here so much." She chuckled, but I really wasn't trying to be amusing. I was done with this crap. In walked the anesthesiologist, once again giving me the whole spiel on what they would do, like I hadn't heard it before. "Let's just go, I need to get this over with," I said. As they wheeled me off to the O.R., I began to vomit. The anesthesiologist stopped the wheelchair and asked me, "Why are you throwing up? Did you eat or drink anything?" I was so annoyed. "No, look at my chart. I'm miscarrying. My body still thinks I'm pregnant," I said. He looked at me almost dumbfounded and said, "Oh, okay I was concerned." I didn't even have the energy to reply. I arrived at the O.R. and there was the doctor waiting, pretty much speechless. I really didn't have anything to say, and neither did he. By now, I definitely knew the routine. We made eye contact, they laid me on the table and he said to me, "Just relax." Of course I was shaking; it's always so damn cold in those operating rooms. "It's going to be over soon," he said. The nurse tossed the warming blanket on top of my legs, and I heard the words, just close your eyes, take a deep breath and count backwards from a hundred . . . never making it past 98.

The surgery was over and they immediately sent me home. All I wanted to do was sleep. My mind and my body were physically drained. My mom watched Rocco, so I was able to completely rest. My mother-in-law lived upstairs, and periodically came down to check on me. I wanted to be alone, to try and absorb what had just happened. Sometimes there are no words that can be said to make it better, silence was needed. A couple of days went by and I was able to relax and build up my strength. My mom would come to pick me up so that I could get out, spend some time at her house and also see my son. Rocco was always guaranteed laughter. He was a bundle of energy from the day he was born. This is what I needed. For Rocco, this was just another sleepover at Mima's and Pipa's. Within a week I had my follow up with the doctor. We had things to discuss. I wanted to know why this was happening. Samples were taken and sent off to pathology. As it turned out there *was* a reason why. The blood work determined that I was carrying a bacteria called Group B streptococcus (GBS), which was leaking into the baby's sack causing me to miscarry. I had never heard of such a condition, another thing I needed to research. *At least we had some sort of an answer*, I thought to myself. The doctor explained that if I did get pregnant again, this would be a high risk factor for me. Apparently, this was a common bacteria that my body was carrying. (Great, just something else to worry about.) As always, he continued to encourage me to not give up. More than anyone else, he knew how much I wanted to give Rocco a sibling. I thought to myself, *Is he crazy?* Not being able to see anything positive here at all, I wasn't feeling hopeful. After doing my homework, I learned that some women are just prone to GBS. I knew this was serious and it could not be taken lightly. This was going to be yet another battle when it came to conceiving. For some strange reason, a small part of me still said, "never give up." I somehow always found the strength to continue trying.

If in life we see God's plan, then we sometimes have to roll with what is thrown at us, right? I learned that life is a journey that builds our strength and character. I think that maybe, just maybe, these hurdles are what prepared me for what life threw my way . . . losing my best friend at the age of twenty-one. It was a reminder that life could take twists and turns, and we need to be prepared for them. A phrase that most of us are familiar with is "what doesn't kill you will make you stronger," and I've found it to be true. I decided I was strong enough to endure, and I would keep trying. This was a decision that only I was able to make. I was the only one who knew what I was capable of. Believing strongly that my body would not let me down, anything was proven to be possible.

Chapter 6

Saying Goodbye

It was 1998, approximately 23 years since grandma had been cancer free. She continued to live her life, enjoying her family and doing things that made her happy. She particularly found so much delight in her grandchildren. They were her pride and joy, especially my three cousins. She always took care of them, while my aunt worked full-time. She lived for her grandchildren. I always made sure that my son Rocco spent plenty of time with her and my grandfather, because he truly brought them so much happiness, as did her other grandchildren. Unfortunately, Grandma and Grandpa were getting older. In fact, Grandma was now eighty-three years old. We all adored her. There was never a dull moment when she was around. They brought excitement whenever they came to visit. She was always my biggest cheerleader. But unfortunately, the struggle to conceive was real and never an easy task. It was a constant uphill battle, but it was the one thing Grandma had always reminded me to stay positive about. And I lived by this. Well, once again by the grace of God, I defeated the odds . . . I was pregnant! Everyone was ecstatic for me, especially Grandma. She would so lightheartedly say, "See, what did I tell you?" Always with that beautiful smile of hers.

If you want to know how I felt, the truth was I didn't feel so thrilled about the situation. It was what I wanted, but I couldn't help feel nervous. Emotionally, I was fearful of the attachment and then possibly having to let go, which was normal after what I'd been through. The months were passing by, and things seemed to be going in the right direction. My doctors had me under close care with weekly visits, due to my high risk. The more time that passed, the more excited I became. I was worrying less about myself, because now I had someone else to worry about–my grandma. She had developed a tumor on her neck. And just like that, our world turned upside down. I kept praying, *please God not again!* Unfortunately, everyone's biggest fear was confirmed, the cancer had returned.

With this news hanging over everyone, it was hard to be happy. My entire family was devastated. We all subconsciously knew where this was going. I knew deep down inside my mom and her sister were somewhat in denial. I couldn't blame them after everything my grandmother had been through. Now, at eighty-three-years-old, how could she possibly fight this? Although we knew she was a warrior, some battles are a force to be reckoned with. And this cancer had a damn agenda of its own. Not only was it back, it was back with a vengeance. Once more, Grandma was a pillar of strength. As heartbroken for her as I was, I looked at her in amazement. She was never anything but courageous to me.

Grandma was becoming weak quickly. The cancer attacked not only her neck but was apparently in her bones as well. It made me sick to my stomach to see her in so much pain, yet she always wore a smile. Did she realize she was entitled to cry and be vulnerable? I only knew her as a fighter. My mom and my aunt were devastated, not willing to believe this was her last battle. They pumped her full of vitamins, but Grandma's body was slowly giving in. This was the fight of her life, that she soon realized she wasn't going to win. I knew my grandmother was going down swinging, because that was who she was.

My mom was a housewife while my aunt worked full-time, and my grandmother needed around-the-clock-care. At this point my mother took my grandparents in. They were determined to keep her home, comfortable and surrounded by her family as long as they could. My mother set her up in my old bedroom, which was downstairs. Grandma could no longer climb the stairs. My mom had now become her mother's caretaker, something she was not prepared for. It wore on her mentally and physically, and was so difficult to watch. There were days when my mom would get frustrated, break down and cry. I know this is what made my mom even more fearful of getting breast cancer. How could it not? Watching someone you love deteriorate every day, knowing the grim reality that is forthcoming would frighten even the bravest. Feeling helpless and angry, she had no choice but to stay strong for her mother. I would go to visit my grandmother everyday with my son Rocco, and try to help my mom as much as I could. I needed to be around to help. I also wanted to be as close as possible. I couldn't believe this was happening again. Knowing how much happiness my son brought my grandmother when he walked through the door, it was all the more important for me to have him see her everyday.

Soon it began to get difficult. Grandma was dependent upon a walker, because the pain was too excruciating for her when she walked. She was a trooper though, always showing us nothing less than her incredible strength and courage. I used to think to myself, *just look at her! How does she do it?* Everyday she got out of bed and my mom would shower her. She would get dressed (never staying in pajamas) do her hair, put on make-up . . . and of course wear her beautiful smile. Grandma certainly had pride in herself, and it showed. Most people would have caved and given up, not my beautiful grandmother. Sometimes my mind played tricks on me. I would walk through the door, see her sitting there and honestly believed she looked okay. Somehow, it felt like a glimmer of hope. It was the little things that brought her happiness at this point, like having her family surround her, especially Rocco. Simple things that made her happy were her favorite lunches: tuna, corn chowder, potatoes and eggs, her love of BBQ chips that I got her hooked on, or a simple card game of war. So, on our daily visits (which I was able to make, because I still had my own business), Rocco and I would bring her favorite BBQ chips. God bless her, she still had an appetite. Rocco was a few months shy of four years old, and he truly adored her. It became routine for us to get up and get ready to go see his Mima. He used to get so excited. There he was, this little peanut holding his Mima's favorite bag of chips. He would walk through the door, and I can still hear that tiny voice saying, "Mima, I'm here, I got your favorite chips for you!" Instantly her face lit up. She got the biggest kick out of him. He knew the routine. He would walk over to the chair, grab her hand and help me and my grandfather get her up, out and moving. "Come on Mima, I'll help you," he would say. It was amazing to see how compassionate an almost four-year-old boy could be. Not understanding the full extent of her illness, he knew something was wrong and always wanted to help. Once we got her up and out of the chair, he would say, "I'll help you push the walker Mima!" He truly filled her heart with joy. This was something she looked forward to every day. Even though I was pregnant, battling morning sickness and juggling my business, I knew it was more important than ever to bring Rocco to see his great-grandmother. I knew these days were priceless.

For some reason, the doctors recommended that a physical therapist come to the house for Grandma. My mom and aunt still held on to the hope that something could make her better. So on one particular day, the physical therapist had her lying on the bed doing some stretches. As I walked into the room, I could see the pain in her eyes as she moved her legs. *Why are they doing this?* I thought to myself. It seemed senseless to me. It was nothing but pain for her to endure. At one point the physical therapist took a break to go speak with my mother in the other room. Alone with my grandmother, she looked at me and said. "Joannie, please make them stop. I can't do this. It's just too painful, please!" This was the first time I had ever seen her so vulnerable. She was crying. My eyes began to fill. "Okay, okay, Grandma I promise I'll go tell mom. Please don't cry!" I didn't know what to do, I hated seeing her like this. I immediately walked into the kitchen and confronted my mother. "Mom listen please, you have to make this stop. This is useless. She's in so much pain. Would you want this for yourself? She's crying in pain!" My mom just looked at me with a blank stare. I could see her eyes filled up with tears. "Please, you know the cancer in her bones. It must be so painful for her, it's torture," I said. Suddenly my mom began to cry. With no words to say, I put my arms around her and held her as she began to sob. My heart was breaking for her. "I know you want to have hope, but this isn't fair to Grandma!" This was a pivotal moment for my mom. It was as if she knew she had to surrender the hope. In a cracking voice she muttered the words, "I know." In her eyes, to acknowledge this meant giving up the fight. She and my aunt were always my grandmother's biggest cheerleaders, but this time the cancer was something much bigger than Grandma.

Things were getting extremely difficult. Grandma was getting worse, and I was not feeling well. My pregnancy was exhausting me. That same week my worst nightmare happened again. I suddenly began to hemorrhage profusely. *What the hell is going to happen next?* I thought. I didn't even know where to turn. *How could I tell my mother, with everything she had on her plate? Never mind telling my grandmother. How would she handle this news from me?* I was around four and half months pregnant, and knew deep down inside that this was not a good sign. I had been down this road before. This was all too much to bear. *How could I possibly lose two of the most precious people in my life . . . my grandmother and my unborn baby?* I knew this was going to be a terrible loss. I was already thinking, *how the hell will I get through this?* My faith was being shaken. I was in danger of losing yet another baby. How could I deliver this news and have my mom endure this too? I had no choice but to tell my mom who was already overwhelmed. I had to get to the doctor as soon as possible. So with limited choices, I called to tell her the news. "Stay calm, and let's pray it's nothing," she said to me. "It's going to be okay. Bring Rocky here first, I'll keep him with me," she continued to say. But I didn't want to burden her and I didn't want her to see me so upset. "No, it's okay. I don't even have time to drop him off, I'll bring him with me." I said. Things were getting progressively worse, quickly. The doctor's office told me to come in immediately. I left it up to my mom to call my father. I called my husband in a panic, who rushed over to meet me. We arrived at the doctor's office only to find out that my regular OB-GYN wasn't in. I had no choice but to see a new doctor in the practice whom I had never met. He had no knowledge of my history and that made me uncomfortable. They immediately put me on the table and performed a sonogram. You could see by the look on his face that he was concerned. He was looking and looking not saying anything at first. "What's going on? Do you hear a heartbeat?" I asked frantically. He had no answer. Then he said, "Well, I think you may have an ectopic pregnancy. I don't see or hear any heart beat." "No I do not have an ectopic pregnancy! Have you even looked at my chart? I was here last week and everything was fine," I yelled. He then looked at me and said "I'm sorry, but I don't see anything, no heartbeat at all." At this point I was enraged. "You don't even know what you're talking about, I want to see my doctor!" I looked at my husband, who was holding Rocco, I swear I thought he was going to knock the doctor out. "Let's go, we'll come back later when my doctor is here. You obviously don't know what the hell you're saying!" I screamed. My regular doctor was due back in about an hour, so we left. I was so damn angry, weak and confused. I kept thinking, *how could he possibly say something that was so stupid?* Storming out of the room I told the receptionist to have the doctor call me as soon as he came in. I just wanted to get the hell out of there! She told me to go home and put my feet up and do nothing, to wait for the doctor's call. I really didn't have many options under the circumstances.

As soon as I arrived home, I gave my mom a call to give her the update. At this point I was beyond weak, and I was starved from not eating. I had to put some sort of food in my body. I grabbed a bagel, toasted up half of it and ate it. No sooner did I swallow my last bite when the phone rang. It was my doctor. He sounded like he was in a panic. "Joanne, where are you right now?" he said. "I'm home, why?" I asked. "You have to meet me at the ER. I just looked over the reports, you are in the middle of a miscarriage, and you are hemorrhaging. There is no time to waste." he said. "Well, the other doctor let me go home, how bad is this?" I began to cry. "You are bleeding out. This is an emergency. We have to get you in and perform a D&C now," he said. Then came the next question. "Have you eaten anything today?" "Yes," I said. "I just ate, I had to. I was so weak from not eating or drinking all day." "Forget the ER, come back to the office immediately," he said. Confused as to why he now wanted me back at the office, we wasted no time and headed over there. The office was only 15 minutes away. We got there quickly. I had no idea what was happening. I kept thinking, *why is he bringing me into the office if he said this was an emergency?* As soon as we arrived and the elevator door opened, I was greeted by the nurse who rushed me directly into a procedure room that was prepped and waiting for my arrival. The doctor came right in. Stunned and unsure of what was happening, I asked, "What's going on here?" Now I was frantic. "I have no choice but to perform the D&C right here," the doctor said as he began to get ready. "I can't put you under anesthesia because you just ate, and we have no time to waste because you are bleeding out." "Wait, what? You want to take this baby out while I'm awake?" I asked. "Are you crazy? How will you even sedate me?" "There is no choice in the matter," the doctor said. "I will give you a local anesthetic and do my best to numb you, but this is do or die." *Numb me*, I thought. My entire body was already numb at that point, with fear! This was one of those moments in life where you just have to pray, suck it up, and hope for the best. When you're in a situation like this, you don't have time to contemplate your decision. The nurse came in to get me undressed and prepared. I still remember the day like it was yesterday. It all happened so quickly, yet it felt like time stood still. Still in disbelief, I could barely process what was happening. This was mentally and physically the hardest thing I ever had to endure. The nurse tried to comfort me and calm me down, but it was impossible. Petrified by the unknown, in the moment all I knew was panic! Trying to talk me through this, the doctor began the procedure. The pain was intense and unbearable. It literally took my breath away. I had to lie there and endure the stabbing pains that were invading my body. The noises that I heard were forever etched in memory. Hearing the sounds of the suction device literally taking out parts of my unborn baby, took a piece of my heart as well. I was asking "Why God, why?" screaming and cursing because I had no control over what was happening. I just wanted it to stop. It was beyond torture. The nurse began to cry as she walked out of the room. (Imagine, it was too much for her. How about me?) Soon my husband followed. He couldn't stand to watch it either. Left lying there alone, it was me and the doctor. I was screaming in pain, but there was no stopping now. He had to finish the procedure. The doctor begged me to keep

50

still, it was almost impossible to do so. I remember pleading with him to please stop. The D&C lasted quite a bit of time, and by the end I was fatigued by the emotions and bleeding. Finally he was done. He said he believed he got everything out. *Everything? You mean my baby?* This was beyond devastating, something that I knew would scar me for the rest of my life. Losing yet another baby, a little girl this time, I was deeply traumatized. Yet, I couldn't blame the doctor. He saved me from bleeding out. With the chain of events, he had no alternative. The procedure was finally over and he packed me to stop the bleeding. I laid there sobbing thinking, *what just happened? I walked into this office pregnant, and now I leave without my sweet baby.*

The doctor had me stay a while. He wanted to watch me to make sure the bleeding had subsided. I remember lying there, lifeless. I had nothing left in me except feelings of hollowness that filled me. There was nothing anyone could say or do to console me. Eventually, they sent me home with strict instructions. I crawled into bed, with no words to speak. All I wanted was to see my mom, but Grandma was too sick to leave alone. I needed her more than ever. I knew Grandma was a priority, so having my mom with me wasn't an option. With nothing but time, all I could do was think. This was the day I began to wonder, *am I done?* I really couldn't endure this anymore. I had one healthy beautiful boy, *why am I pushing this? Was it so important to give my son a sibling? Maybe this was God's way of telling me, enough! How much more could my body endure?* This was beyond damaging for me. I can't even begin to tell you what the experience had done to me emotionally. This was forever imprinted on my soul–the pain, the sounds, the anguish. I have only shared this with two people during my lifetime, not many know what I went through. Can you imagine having your unborn child ripped out of you? Never getting the chance to lay her to rest respectfully? This left a void in my heart forever! Something I had to learn to shelf and live with. This being an extremely emotional time I grieved alone, in my own mind. I never confided in anyone. Not even my mom. She was grieving herself. I knew this was something that I had to mentally pull through on my own. Unless you walked in my shoes, how could anyone possibly understand how I felt? To add to this traumatic experience, I was also losing the most special person in my life . . . my grandmother.

As the days went by, I couldn't do much except take it easy and relax. I had a lot of healing to do. Psychologically it was extremely difficult. I felt like everywhere I turned I saw darkness. My mom was struggling as well. It was a troublesome for all of us. She had so much on her shoulders. It was a trying time for her. Yet, she somehow found a way to stay strong for all of us. I began to heal, and there were days that I was better off going to my mom's where she could help me with Rocco (besides, I got to spend time with my ailing grandmother). It lifted her spirits to have her family around.

Rocco was too little to understand the circumstances surrounding the loss of his sibling. I slowly stopped talking about Rocco's brother or sister that he was so excited to welcome, out of sight out of mind. He was a ray of sunshine for all of us. I would hold him tight, constantly reminding myself what a blessing he was. He was the sweetest, most compassionate little boy. Sensing something was wrong, he would make us laugh. It was what we all needed at this time in our lives.

Time was precious now. Even when my grandmother knew there was no hope for herself, she would somehow find the words to console me. She continued to reminded me to never give up on hope. How could a woman who was losing her life to cancer tell me not to lose hope? She was so incredible and inspiring. Yet, she didn't know what I was thinking. *I'm done. I refuse to go through this again. Truly, how much can one take?* I can still feel her arms around me, playing with my hair, just letting me know how much she loved me. I can smell her Jean Nate perfume when I close my eyes. As I held her, my emotions were swirling. *Was I crying for the baby I just lost, or because I was about to lose my grandmother?* Once again I questioned. *Why God, why? Why is our faith constantly being tested? When do we get a break in this family?*

The same week of my miscarriage, we had a family function that we were all invited to. I was in no condition to attend, nor was my grandmother. Grandma at this point felt so embarrassed, she couldn't possibly go to a party in her condition. She was using a walker and had issues going to the bathroom. Everything was a huge struggle for her. I suggested to my mom that I would stay behind with Grandma, while she, Grandpa and my dad went to the party. I really was in no condition to go anywhere, not mentally or physically. My mother wasn't comfortable with that, because I couldn't lift or do anything physical. It made her nervous to leave me with Grandma. I somehow convinced her to go and told her it would be fine. The day of the party arrived, and Grandma was upset she couldn't attend. As my mom was getting ready to go, Grandma looked at me and said "Can you help me to the table? I want to fill out the card for your mom to bring to the party." I got her over to the chair and she sat down. She grabbed the pen and all of a sudden began to cry. "Look at me, I can't even write!" she said. Her hands were shaking profusely. My heart was broken. This was yet another rare incident when she cried and was vulnerable. "Grandma, it's okay, I'll help you, don't cry," I said. She just looked at me with tears streaming down her face, and said, "Thank you my Joannie, I love you." "I love you too Grandma," I said. This was heart wrenching for me. Knowing how real this was, I didn't feel it would be long now. That night Grandma, little Rocco and I ordered Chinese food for dinner. We sat and watched all her favorite shows. While my parents took Grandpa for a couple of hours to the party, I managed to get her to play her favorite card game, "May I". We even had some laughs that night. She was a trooper and so brave. I tried to keep her occupied, knowing these moments were so precious. Ironically that night, she needed me and I needed her. Aware of what I had gone through that week, Grandma constantly reminded me to stay hopeful. Always having her encouragement was so special. I couldn't imagine what life was going to be without Grandma, for all of us.

Every day became more and more of a struggle for my mom and my aunt. They were watching their beautiful mother fade. My aunt and cousins came as frequently as they could. My aunt worked full-time and didn't live close by, but together she and my mom continued to care for their mother as best they could, with the determination of keeping her home. Watching my mom exhaust herself, I said to her one day, "Mom, why don't you and Dad go down to the Jersey Shore for a night and I will stay with Grandma." "No," she immediately said, "You and Grandpa can't possibly handle her, it's way too much." But I knew that I could. I also knew that she needed to escape for a night. With a little convincing and a lot of hesitation she agreed to go. Planning the night, she laid out my grandma's itinerary, listing everything that needed to be done. Then they then headed out. "Okay Grams, it's just me, you and Grandpa," I said. She just smiled. We ordered food, watched some TV, and again played her favorite card game. No matter what condition she was in, she was always up for a good game of cards. The day passed without incident and it was time to put Grandma down to bed. Grandpa and I brought her into the bathroom, where we washed her up, brushed her teeth, and then headed to the bedroom. We sat her on the bed. "Okay Grandpa, I can take it from here," I said. Closing the door behind him, I walked over to Grandma. She had a sad look on her face. She was just so frail. "What's the matter, Grams," I asked. "I can do this," she said. "I can undress myself." "Grandma please, you can't even lift your arms, let me help you," I said. It was at that moment I realized she was holding back. This was the first time she was going to expose herself to me. I had never seen her "flat." "It's okay, just let me help you lift your arms." She wasn't even wearing her prosthesis bra. For the first time, I saw her scars. Her eyes began to fill with tears. I knew I had to stay strong, she always showed me nothing but strength! I kept telling myself, *don't cry Jo . . . DO NOT cry!* Without words I looked at her, and at that very moment I realized what she had endured. For the first time, I understood the magnitude of breast cancer (the beast as I called it) and what it had done to her. I had never seen anything like it before. Nor did I ever see her like this. She had to be able to feel what I was thinking. "Grandma, you know what?" I said. She looked at me, sitting there helplessly with tears in her eyes, "You are my hero!" As I tried to hold back the tears, Grandma grabbed my wrist with one hand, and with her other hand she held my arm and began to kiss my arm up and down. She muttered the words, "Oh my Joannie, I love you. Please don't leave me, stay with me." The tears began to flow uncontrollably down my cheeks, I couldn't even see. "Grandma, I will stay by your side until your last breath, I promise! I love you so much! Please don't cry." I sat on the edge of the bed and I hugged her tightly. I never wanted to let her go. If I could have taken her pain away at that moment, I would have. My heart was broken for her. I tucked Grandma in and gave her kisses and hugs, placed the pillows all around her, and made sure she was comfortable. As I walked out of the room, I prayed and asked God to not let her suffer anymore, she didn't deserve it. She had been through so much in her life. I walked into the bathroom and shut the door behind me. Grabbing a towel to cover my mouth, I sat there and cried uncontrollably. I didn't want her to hear me, my heart was shattered. I felt so much pain for her, I just wanted to make it stop. These past weeks were, for sure, a test on my emotions. I was going to lose this perfect person that I adored. Life was testing my faith. Although spending this night with Grandma was priceless, it was at the same time upsetting.

With the passing days, Grandma got progressively worse and needed hospital care. At the time I lived in Oceanside, N.Y., and this was where the hospital was located. My mom had a phobia of hospitals, and tended to avoid them at all costs. I was basically a five minute car drive away, so I could help my mom with whatever she needed. In the days that followed, family was in and out of the hospital to visit Grandma. My mom would cook some of her favorite foods and have me bring it up to her. One day in particular, I walked into the hospital room with her lunch and Grandma was out cold sleeping. I sat down quietly and began to flick through the television channels waiting for her to wake. All of a sudden I heard Grandma mumbling, "Mom, Mom, Mom, Helen." I stood up and tried to wake her. "Grandma, wake up. It's me, are you okay? Wake up!" With a smile on her face she calmly opened her eyes, turned to me and said, "I just saw my mother and my sisters. It was so beautiful." This made me happy. Why? Because I was always one who believed that when we pass, our loved ones are there waiting. "No doubt Grandma, I am sure they are all here with you," I said. She just lay there so calmly, smiling again. "Come on Grams, let's sit you up. I have food for you." My mom had made her favorite corn chowder. That day I was able to get her to eat some. By this stage we knew it was only a matter of days. The family just cherished every moment we had left with her. I shared with Grandma that I would be training to walk in the 60 mile Avon Breast Cancer walk in her honor. I had participated in so many of these walk-athons in years past, but this was going to be a tough one! It was going to take vigorous training, to walk 20 miles a day, for three days straight! Walking along the Hudson, from Bear Mountain to Central Park, I had to keep in the forefront that every step I would take would remind me of her. She was happy when I told her, and inquisitive to know more. Grandma knew how much I loved her, and that I was doing this in her honor. I made her laugh when I told her I would be wearing a shirt with her picture on it. We even joked when I said, "Just make sure to watch over me and give me a kick in the ass when I want to quit!"

Our family was gathered around her bedside knowing that the time of her departure was nearing. She was definitely surrounded by so much love in her last days. There were many tears, some laughter because of the good memories, and many people praying for the end of her suffering. The doctors began to make her comfortable with drugs, so she could peacefully drift away. We would order food and eat in her room, so that no one would have to leave her side. None of us wanted Grandma to be alone when she passed. I promised her that I wouldn't leave her side and those were my intentions. The next morning the nurse came in to check on her vitals, everything seemed to be okay.

There was no sign of her declining. The nurse then turned to everyone in the family and said, "Why don't you all go home, eat, get some rest and come back? Her vitals look stable." She could clearly see the exhaustion on everyone's faces. So with a little convincing my aunt and my cousins headed back out east. They lived about an hour away. Everyone began to scatter, we were all exhausted. My parents lived much closer, only about 15 minutes from the hospital, so they stayed a little longer. The only people left in the room at this point were my parents, Grandpa and me. Grandpa was passed out in the recliner. He was so sleep deprived we couldn't even wake him. He was becoming lethargic, he needed to rest. Even if we were able to wake him, he would have never wanted to leave her side. His sweetheart was lying in that bed. Then my mom turned to me and said, "Why don't you go home for a bit? I'll stay here with Grandpa, and when you come back I'll go home for a little while." Immediately I replied, "No, you go, I will stay with her." I knew what I promised Grandma, I wasn't going anywhere. Mom was hesitant to leave, especially knowing her sister had left to run home for a bit. She wanted either herself or her sister with my grandma. But she and my father decided they lived close enough, so they were going to leave and come right back. My mind was made up, I was staying! With that, my parents headed out. No sooner did they get to the elevator, I noticed Grandma's breathing was becoming shallow. I jumped up and I immediately called for the nurse. As she was listening to Grandma's heart I tried to wake my grandfather, but he was still lethargic in the chair. It was so crazy how I just couldn't wake him up. "GRANDPA, GRANDPA, come on GET UP!" I was shaking him. The nurse looked at me and said, "I'm sorry, she is going." "What!" I screamed, "NO, please go get my parents, they just went down the hallway!" As the nurse ran to get my parents, I tried to wake Grandpa again. He just wouldn't respond. I walked over to the other side of the bed, I wrapped my arms around my grandmother's head, leaned into her ear, and with tears uncontrollably streaming down my face, I whispered. "It's okay Grandma, go be at peace now. We all love you . . . I love you! No more pain, I love you so much!" I repeatedly said these words. Watching her take her last breath, I held her tight. I had felt this heartache before with the death of my daughter and here I was again. As my parents came running back into the room, I was crying, "Mom she's gone, she's gone!" At this point, I guess from all the chaos, Grandpa suddenly came to. Helping him up off the chair, he sat on the bed holding her and cried uncontrollably. My heart was breaking for him, and my mom as well. I remember thinking . . . *no more pain Grandma, no more suffering, just peace now.* With nothing left to feel, think, hope or say, we all just surrounded this beautiful courageous woman that we all loved so much. A warrior who was a mother, wife, sister, aunt, grandmother, and great grandmother. With the word of this reaching my aunt and cousins, they immediately returned to the hospital to say goodbye. I remember just sitting there feeling numb. This was a hard hit in life for all of us, especially my mom and my aunt. To see how heartbroken they were, pained me even more. Trying to imagine the loss of a parent, and what they were feeling was foreign to me. My first thought was, *how am I going to explain this to my son Rocco, who loved his Mima so much? How do I tell him that Mima is in heaven now? How will he ever be able to understand that there will be no more bringing her favorite chips? No more daily visits, no more helping her out of the chair . . . no more Mima.* That day the earth had lost one of the most courageous, inspiring, kindred souls. A very determined and loving person, who displayed nothing but strength to her family. She instilled in all of us, that fear was not an option. Heaven had gained yet another angel. I lost an incredible role model, one who I adored . . . my beautiful grandmother. From this moment on, I knew that the women in this family needed to be self advocates by being pro-active. Not yet understanding just how close this beast was to us.

August 11th, 1998, may you forever Rest in Peace Grandma. We lost a piece of our hearts when you left us.

Chapter 7

Walking In The Right Direction

As I promised my grandmother, the next summer August 1999, I walked the 60 mile breast cancer walk. The training was rigorous. My girlfriend and I decided we would do this together. She was an oncology nurse, and had lost many patients to breast cancer. She had seen her fair share of loss. Once we decided we would conquer this, we both knew we needed to prepare for this 20 mile-a-day walk. We tried to walk at least 4-8 miles a day, breaking in our special sneakers that we would wear for the event. Not only did we have to prepare physically, but mentally as well. The itinerary was a three-day event, pitching and sleeping in two-man tents, showering in portable showers in the cold nights, and walking from Bear Mountain, New York, down the Hudson all the way to Central Park. This was no joke. Talk about a team of volunteers. There were doctors, chiropractors, masseuses, chefs . . . you name it, they were there. (Including one very important crew, the one that transported our Porta-Potties wherever we went. You want to talk about humbling.) We walked with so many survivors, and many people like myself who lost loved ones to the beast. We bought all sorts of breast cancer gear to wear for the event. As promised, there was one special shirt that I made, with Grandma's face on the front that would be front and center. One of the stipulations, in order to participate in the event, required us to raise money for research. All in all, I believe it was $1,800. I was so proud that I was able to raise $2,500. I knew this was for a good cause, something so near to my heart. We were excited, nervous, and we were fully committed.

After months of consistently training, the special weekend was finally here. On the first day, all the walkers and helpers were bused up to a hotel on Bear Mountain where we spent the night preparing and meeting many amazing people. It was a night to connect, get to know each other, lift each other up and get pumped for the challenge. When the going got tough, we had to remember that our loved ones went through much worse. The long walk was a small sacrifice that we would have to endure. The next morning we had to rise really early, pack all of our belongings and hand them over to the crew, who transported our things from site to site. We were each allowed one duffel bag, packed with three days of clothes inside zip lock baggies so they wouldn't get damp. Excited, we hopped on the buses, and drove through thick dense scary fog to get to the start-up location. As we unloaded off the buses, the fog broke and the sun began to rise. It turned out to be a beautiful August morning. As we got off the buses, the music was blasting. People were cheering us on to get us pumped and excited. It reminded me that we were all in this together. I can't even begin to explain the electrifying atmosphere that was in the air. It was something I had never experienced before, a new adventure. All I could think about was my beautiful grandmother, hoping that she was looking down at me and I was making her proud. I was constantly gazing up at the sky saying, "This is for you, Grandma!" After eating a good breakfast, we were ready to rock and roll. We headed out. With the music blasting and people cheering, I thought to myself, *wow, this is incredible!* My girlfriend and I were each other's biggest cheerleaders, always encouraging and pushing each other through with a lot of laughs (and sometimes tears). As we walked through the towns, people were lined up throughout offering us food, snacks and drinks. We walked all along the Hudson, occasionally stopping to take in the beautiful views, but we knew there was no time to waste. Barreling through each day, I found it strenuous. For some strange reason I couldn't understand, I was feeling a little sluggish. We had trained so hard for this. When it seemed to get difficult, I simply reminded myself of the pain my grandmother endured. This was what kept me going. Towards the end of the first 20 miles, our feet were killing us and our fingers were swollen from the heat. It was a scalding hot day. I told my girlfriend that I was feeling light headed. I knew something wasn't right. I was literally pushing myself to the finish line. By the time I made it to the end of the walk and arrived at the tents, I began to feel really nauseous. Since she was a nurse, she knew right away that I was dehydrated, but I couldn't understand why. I drank a lot of water, but one thing I didn't drink was Gatorade, which had the electrolytes. Concerned, she took me to the medical tent to get checked out. Sure enough, I was dehydrated. They laid me down for a bit and filled me with fluids until I began to feel better. Calling it an early night, knowing what was ahead for tomorrow, we took cold showers in portable shower stalls, pitched the tent and crawled in for a good night's sleep. Let me tell you, that in itself was an adventure. Laughing until the tears were rolling down our faces, we finally passed out. We were exhausted.

The second day proved to be another hot August day. It didn't matter to us, we were so motivated and excited to get going. We woke up, took down our tent and headed out to grab some breakfast. All fueled up, we began the walk. As we headed into the day, again I was feeling sluggish and tired. Still dealing with some nausea, I kept saying to my girlfriend, "I don't understand, I trained so hard for this. Why do I not have stamina? This should be so easy for me." I was an avid walker to begin with, and always had plenty of energy. Thinking that I still may be a little dehydrated, I made sure to drink plenty of Gatorade that day. Using my grandmother for my forefront of inspiration, I reminded myself of the hurdles she had to jump over in her lifetime. Along the way we made many friends, and so many people inspired us as well. One gentleman in particular, is cemented in my memory. He was an 81-year-old man who walked the entire route with a cane. We befriended him and he shared that he had just lost his wife to breast cancer. He was walking in her memory. *Imagine that! What an incredible person*, we both thought. He inspired us to push through and not give up. That's what we did, nauseated or not. We did it! We made another 20 miles! We were exhausted, our feet were blistered, but we were also feeling so proud of our accomplishment. We grabbed some dinner, took another cold shower, and pitched the tents in the rain. We crawled in, laid there and talked about how amazing this experience truly was. Eventually we passed out from sheer exhaustion. Even though we were completely spent, we were super excited about tomorrow . . . the finish line.

By the third day, we didn't know how we were going to endure another day of walking, yet we were determined. We reminded ourselves of all the pain that our loved ones went through, and kept that in sight. Although our feet were in agony and we were struggling to make another 20 miles, our adrenaline was rushing. This was the finish line day. As we were prepared to head off, my girlfriend and I looked at each other and I said, "We got this girlfriend, let's do it!" *What's another 20 miles? Huh, a piece of cake, I thought.* Two days of pitching tents in the rain, sleeping on cots, showering in portable shower stalls, using portable potties, endless laughs along with some tears . . . we wouldn't have had it any other way. As we got closer to Manhattan, the streets were flooded with people cheering us on. It was so moving to see that people were really listening and paying attention to the cause. *We needed to make strides to stop this cancer,* I thought. Again I felt like I had to push myself, making sure to stay hydrated. We could not wait to get to the grand finale. As we approached Central Park, the atmosphere was lit. There were balloons everywhere, music blasting and people cheering and chanting for us. It was such an emotional moment, especially for me. Crossing the finish line, while wearing the t-shirt with my beautiful grandmother's face on it . . . was beyond moving. I couldn't help but cry. "I hope I made you proud Grandma, this was for you!" I told her. My girlfriend and I were so proud of ourselves and each other. We hugged with tears of joy and feelings of accomplishment. This had definitely been a mental and physical challenge! We had to constantly remind ourselves to not give up as well as encourage each other. I can't begin to express how honored I felt walking with so many fighters, and so many people who lost their loved ones to breast cancer. Being a part of this journey for four days was like being on a retreat. Everyone was nice to each other, and we always looked out for one another. There were no curse words to be heard, no arguing, no competitiveness of any sort . . . just kindness. *The way it should always be,* we thought. To be there and be a part of this event was extremely special.

By the time I returned home that night I was completely exhausted, and quite honestly, I was still feeling nauseous. I called my friend and told her how I was feeling. I wasn't getting any better. Her response . . . "I think you may be pregnant!" *No way!* I thought. Honestly, after what I had gone through with the last miscarriage, I wasn't even trying to get pregnant. Nor was I thinking about it! In fact, my doctor had given me a script for fertility pills that I had filled months ago. They sat on the window sill . . . I never even took them! Can you blame me? I had mixed emotions about trying again. Part of me was truly done. In fact, the possibility of a hysterectomy was already being discussed. Yet, my doctor continued to encourage me to never stop trying. I knew I never wanted to go through another hardship of a miscarriage again. Even so, I always remembered the words my grandmother would say, "If God wants you to have a baby, then you will," which never allowed me to lose sight of my faith. A couple of days went by, and I finally told my mom how I was feeling. She too agreed that I may be pregnant. I procrastinated taking a test because I was scared, but I knew I had to find out what was going on. Curious to know, I decided to pick up a test at the store. My periods were never normal, I couldn't go by that. I was suspicious because of the way I felt. I took the test, laid it down on the bathroom counter and walked away. Uncertain of what it would be, I didn't know if I truly wanted it to be positive. My fear was over shadowing the possibilities. Walking back into the bathroom to take a look, there it was, once

AGAIN . . . POSITIVE!!! Talk about a bag of mixed emotions. I was happy, scared, overwhelmed all at the same time! Honestly, I was more scared crap than anything else. I immediately said to God, "Please don't take this baby from me, please!" I don't think I could have handled another loss at this point. In my heart I felt something different about this pregnancy. I hadn't focused on having another baby, it happened unplanned and naturally. I couldn't help but feel that my grandmother sent me a beautiful gift. She always knew how much I wanted a second child. I was constantly thanking God, and Grandma. "Thank you," I kept saying. I reminded myself that I needed to stay positive, and keep a hold on my faith. This was yet another miracle for me. In disbelief, I immediately called my doctor and ran over to do the test in the office. The doctor was thrilled for me, yet he recognized my look of concern, rightfully so. The doctor explained that I was at high risk of GBS (Group B Streptococcus), and I would be going for weekly visits throughout the pregnancy. Knowing that this was the cause for the other miscarriages, they would constantly monitor and test me. My emotions were boiling over. I was excited and fearful all at the same time. I only told my immediate family. My parents were over the moon for me! My mom always tried to keep me positive. I wasn't showing much excitement. I didn't want to bond with my baby just yet. I didn't want to get my hopes up, and then be disappointed. I didn't tell people until I was about five months pregnant or so. I hid it well. I was so sick with this pregnancy, I hardly showed until about five and half months. I didn't want to have to explain myself if something happened again. Since I owned a business, I wanted to keep it quiet for a bit. Months went by, I continued with my weekly visits and things seemed to be okay. *Who was I kidding? I was completely bonding with this baby already, how could I not?* As a mother, I immediately had this connection. My excitement grew bigger along with my belly! The vomiting was really getting on my nerves! It was so bad in fact, that I only gained 14 pounds with the entire pregnancy, and I developed esophagitis from all the acidity. 'Til this day, I will tell you that it was all worth it. As I got closer to the nine month mark, I knew it was going to be okay. I couldn't help but think that my angel grandmother was always with me. Knowing how much of a blessing this baby was truly excited me. The family was filled with enthusiasm for me, and for my brother and his wife who were expecting only weeks after me. Finally, some happiness was surrounding us. I was thrilled that Rocco was going to have a baby brother or sister. After an emotional year, this family was about to become a family of four!

On April 27th, 2000, God blessed me with another miracle baby. Christian Joseph was born, at 3:15 am, weighing in at 8 pounds 2 oz. This was an abundance of happiness for me, once again beating the odds! Holding this beautiful baby boy in my arms was something I thought could never happen. Truly a gift from above. He was perfect, with sandy brown hair and chubby cheeks. His big brother Rocco was over the moon. Just shy of 5 years old, Rocco understood how special Christian was. I could not begin to express my feelings as I held my son. The struggles were trying at times, but I never gave up on my faith. I felt complete, and undefeated. But most of all, I knew I was blessed. God was good!

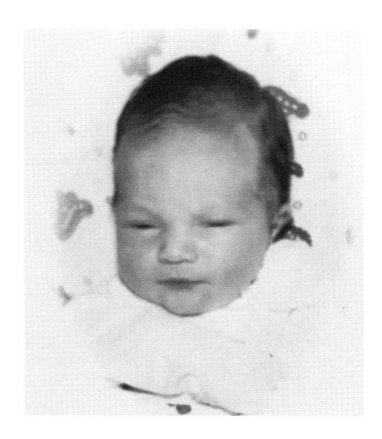

Chapter 8

The Decision

Having my two boys was truly a blessing, and it had taken significant effort to get to this place in life. Endometriosis sometimes could get better with pregnancy, but in my case it was the complete opposite. With every pregnancy it got worse. It wasn't something I was willing to deal with anymore. I felt I had paid my dues between endless laparoscopic surgeries, D&Cs and miscarriages. I was at an end, especially knowing that high levels of estrogen would play a role in an increased risk of breast cancer. Having had many discussions with my doctor, even before I had my second son, I knew that a hysterectomy was inevitable. Did I want more children? Of course I did. But it became too risky. I couldn't believe we were already seriously talking about a hysterectomy, I was so young. I seemed to be mirroring my mom's history. She was only thirty-one, when she had a hysterectomy. Here I was just as young, at thirty-two-years-old, eerily genetically following in her footsteps. My mom and I had intense discussions about the risks of having a hysterectomy at such a young age. My mom would always say, "You'll be okay. I'm an example of an early hysterectomy and I am doing just fine." She constantly reassured me of this. This was a decision that had to be made sooner rather than later. And who better to take this advice from, but my mom. She lived it, and was now watching her daughter go through it. Neither one of us realized how soon this would need to be done.

After Christian was born, my periods immediately got heavier and more painful. I knew exactly what was brewing. Deep down inside I was very concerned. I avoided what needed to be done, procrastinating and just carrying on with life, as if it would just go away. Christian was such a sweet addition to our family, all I wanted to do was enjoy him. All the while my doctor was watching me closely, reminding me that there was a decision to be made soon. Honestly, I was doing my best to avoid the inevitable. He noticed that I was developing another "chocolate cyst," and this was very concerning to him. Time was ticking. Christian was only seven months old and I couldn't focus or wrap my head around this surgery. How could I possibly handle a five year old, a newborn and surgery?

The day was November 15, 2000. I was out and about doing some early Christmas shopping and it was also my son Rocco's birthday in a couple of days. I wanted to pick up a few last minute gifts for him. When I woke up that morning I knew I wasn't well, but I really didn't know why. Brushing it off, I ran to a local store to do some shopping. As I walked into the store, I felt something happen. Before I knew it, I was doubled over in the most excruciating pain, one that I was familiar with. Barely making it back to my car, I managed to drive myself home, which was about five minutes away. I ran into the bathroom, to find I was bleeding profusely. *This could not be good*, I thought. I had been down this road too many times. I knew this was urgent. I immediately called the doctor who told me to meet him at the local ER as soon as possible. It was as if he knew what had happened. I called my mother to arrange for her to pick up the boys only to find out she had gone away for the night. I was beside myself, I really needed her with me. Luckily, my mother-in-law was able to help. I left my boys with her, as there was no time to waste. Arriving at the hospital, I was greeted by my doctor. I knew the conversation we were going to have was not going to be pleasant. He immediately ordered some tests. The chocolate cyst had burst. Even though I had been through this before, I knew this time I was facing something much bigger. The doctor sat at the edge of my bed and said, "We need to talk, this is serious. I need to know if you are done trying to have more children?" It was the dreaded million dollar question that had been hanging over my head. I knew this decision I was about to make, like my mother did at a young age, would ask me to give up one of the most valuable things I owned . . . my womanhood, my ability to create life. Easier said than done. This wasn't something you decided like you would when you turned off a light switch. This was very final. Once I took this step, there would be no turning back. I couldn't even speak, never mind answer the question. I choked up, and tried to control the tears and the pain that had crept up to my shoulders. Honestly, this wasn't a totally new conversation. We had spoken about this, and I knew this day was coming. It was my decision and my decision only, but I wanted to speak to my mom for reassurance. There was no way of getting in touch with her. Unfortunately, the decision needed to be made now, I already knew her take on this. Much like her hysterectomy decision to stop the suffering, I needed to do the same. There really was no time to waste. Trying to pull myself together, I began to ask what I thought, at the time, were the ridiculous questions. In hindsight, all I was doing was reassuring myself. Even though we had discussed the risks and benefits before, I asked anyway.

Will I immediately go through menopause?

Will I get fat?

Will I grow facial hair?

How about hot flashes?

Bone loss?

He actually chuckled at me. "Well yes, I am basically ripping out all of your hormones at once, but no you will not get fat or grow facial hair. We will have to do a complete hysterectomy, with nothing left behind. Your incisions will be hip to hip. This will require a significant period of recovery, but this is how it has to be done. I have to go in and clean out all the scar tissue that developed after years of endometriosis," he said. "The only thing we will leave is your cervix to give you some bladder support." At this point I was hemorrhaging and the pain was excruciating, I could barely breathe. This was probably the worst it had ever been. This disease didn't play, happening only seven months after I gave birth. This was it! The decision had to be made, and that's exactly what I did . . . I gave him the go ahead. One of the most difficult days of my life, truly. Counting my blessings, I knew how lucky I was to have my beautiful boys. It was time to call it quits. Once we finalized the paperwork, it was like an elephant was lifted off my back. Besides, the pain was so bad, I didn't care what they had to do. I just wanted it to stop.

The surgery was set for the first time slot the next morning. I was in so much pain, I kept saying to the nurse, "I think I am going to die." I was bleeding internally and I was frightened. I was a wreck. I really needed to speak to my mom. I needed to hear her voice, and see my dad who was always my sense of calm. I was petrified, and riddled with pain everywhere. Eventually the nurse had to give me some sedation. Between the pain and anticipation, I was going out of my mind. Even with the drugs they gave me, I still found it difficult to relax. The nurses came in frequently throughout the night to check on me. I begged them to call my doctor. I wanted the surgery that night. She assured me I was okay and to try and rest. I kept thinking that I was going to bleed out. By now, I was mentally drained and wanted this nightmare to be over. Nighttime had turned to morning, and the sun was finally up. I don't know how I made it through the night, that's how bad the pain was. Finally, the doctor walked in. As they began to prep me, he went over all the logistics of the surgery. I didn't even give a crap at this point, I just wanted them to knock me out already. I don't think I heard a word he said, quite honestly. As they wheeled me off to the O.R., the tears were streaming. The doctor held my hand, tried to comfort me, and reminded me that I was in good hands. "Okay, I'll see you in the O.R., you're going to be fine," he said. The O.R. was freezing cold as usual, and I was shaking uncontrollably. The nurses and doctors were all around me doing their thing. They put the warming blanket on me, began to push the meds through my veins, and one of the nurses held my hand and said, "Take some deep breaths, when you wake it will all be over." This was the most relief I had in hours and I welcomed it. I didn't try to fight it, I closed my eyes and left it in God's hands.

Surgery was about 4 hours long. I remember the nurses trying to wake me up, but I was just so weak and tired. All I wanted to do was sleep. Before I knew it I found myself in the recovery room. All of a sudden, I heard the voice I had wanted to hear, "JoJo, JoJo, open your eyes, it's Mom!" I opened my eyes. There she was holding my hand, and my dad was standing right next to her. I remember her eyes were bloodshot and filled with tears that she was trying to hold back. "I needed you," I began to cry, "I didn't know what to do!" She didn't know what to say except to assure me I made the right decision, knowing that at thirty-one she was faced with the same situation. "Come on, don't cry, it's going to be okay. You have those two beautiful boys at home. That's all you need now," she said. I remember being in so much pain. I was wrapped like a mummy, yet I was able to find some humor. "No it's not, I am already having a hot flash!" No joke, I was! Literally sweating, she got me a cool rag for my head as she started to laugh. "Mom, how will I do this with a five-year-old and seven-month-old?" I asked. "Don't worry, I will help you," she said. Of course, it would have been silly of me to think anything different. She was constantly there for me. Then all of a sudden I began to cry. "What's wrong?" Mom asked me. "I just realized tomorrow is Rocco's birthday, and I won't be home to celebrate with him," I sobbed. (Of course this was probably my non-hormonal body kicking in already.) It killed me to know I couldn't be home with my son for his fifth birthday. "Don't worry, I'll get him a cake and have everyone by me. When you get out we will celebrate again, I promise", she said. "We'll bring him to see you tomorrow. Come on, don't cry." She was just the most amazing mother anyone could ever have. As I began to calm down, the doctor walked in to check on me and explain how the surgery went. "How are you feeling?" he asked. "Well, right now, I'm having a huge hot flash, and I'm an emotional mess," I said. He laughed, "Yes, I just removed all your hormones, so that makes complete sense," he said making light of the situation. *Great, this was just the beginning,* I thought, *menopause at thirty two! Oh joy!* I really had no idea what I was in for. But one thing I did know, I wasn't going to miss those painful periods at all. "You won't regret your decision. The endometriosis had spread, you had scar tissue everywhere. It was dispersed throughout and needed to be done." he said. "This will give you a better quality of life. And the best achievement is your two healthy boys! You definitely beat the odds Joanne. Just look how far you have come," he said. And deep down inside, I did know how lucky I was. This was definitely a difficult day physically and emotionally, but with all the love and support I had, I got through it. The sun rose and it was Rocco's birthday. My mom grabbed both my boys, the birthday gifts and came up to see me. I was so happy to see them both. I kept thinking, *how will I be able to lift a seven-month-old* when I go home? I had a long road of healing ahead of me, and knew it was going to be a challenge.

Mentally, the hysterectomy proved to be very difficult because I realized with every passing day, that this was final. Whenever I would get down and depressed, all I had to do was look at my two miracle babies, and I knew it was all going to be okay. I also reminded myself, after years of suffering, of the pain free days that were ahead. One of the many things the doctor was right about was that it was going to be a long and slow recovery. As the days passed I began to heal. After about a week in the hospital, with frequent visits from my family and my boys, it was time to head home. Within two weeks or so after arriving home I began to work again. This was a very busy time at my dance studio. It was the time of year when we were measuring and ordering costumes.There was no time to sit back, I had to get better quickly. It was part of my personality to just keep going.

I wasn't one to sit idle. I couldn't teach, but I was still able to run the business. Weeks and then months passed. I was healing nicely, but the reality was that it would take about a year to fully recover. Physical healing wasn't the only thing that was needed, I also needed to mentally heal. This was all taxing, because of many years of mental and physical strain on my body. These were my own struggles. I didn't let this show, I had to do the healing within myself. Returning back to work, quite honestly, was the best thing as it kept me occupied. It was a great coping mechanism for me, to carry on and do what I loved best, manage my dance studio. As they say . . . time heals all. The most treasured lesson of my life thus far, is to always continue to hold on to faith, if we let go of faith then we have no hope.

Chapter 9

Years Gone By

Years went by and my health was finally in check. The uphill climb was a little easier. With the passage of time I was enjoying my boys, living life free of pain, and immersed in my dance studio. I knew how priceless my family was, and I was grateful and felt blessed for what I had. They say that time heals, and it did. I no longer focused on what I couldn't have, but focused on what I did have. I also no longer focused on days of pain, but I enjoyed the freedom from pain. Everything I fought for in the end was something I would have done over again. These boys were my life. I always considered myself a person of determination. I constantly dusted myself off and got right back up again. I learned that life was about challenges, and we have to be ready for the battle. My genetic footprints were a constant reminder of the potential battles to come. I never let my guard down, and always stayed aware of the risk of breast cancer.

It was something I never let slip from my mind. I kept myself informed of new strides, walked in many fundraisers, and stayed diligent with my breast examinations. I also constantly drilled the importance of early detection into my mom. It was a goal of mine to motivate her, but she wouldn't listen. In fact, the grim reminder of our genetics was about to hit our family hard once again. It was around 2008 when my mom learned her sister was diagnosed with breast cancer. If my memory is clear, it was close to the fall and I was actually in the middle of organizing a breast cancer fundraiser, when my mother called me to tell me the news. She was crying hysterically. "Joanne, you're not going to believe this" . . . she said, and I almost didn't. This beast had attacked another woman in our family. I loved my aunt very much, we were very close. I was in shock, or was I really? We knew the possibility of it passing down genetically was high. I was sick for my mom. I knew right away what she was thinking. My mom would not survive another loss to this disease, especially her sister whom she cherished and clung to as her only sibling. I just couldn't believe this was happening. *Why?* This again was a pivotal moment for me. I needed to be more proactive. I needed to get my mother on board as well. The power of genetics was truly a force to be reckoned with. Well aware of how I mirrored my mom and grandmother, it was beginning to frighten me more and more.

My mom truly was beside herself. She was so worried about her sister. Can you blame her? My aunt had recently lost her husband. She lived about an hour away and my mom was no longer able to drive. My mother was upset that she wasn't living in closer proximity to her sister. She knew that my aunt needed her support, they only had each other. She also knew what lay ahead for my aunt. After going through it with my grandmother,

JOANNE AMERUOSO

they were both very aware. My dad made sure that my mom could be there for her sister. And my aunt knew she could count on them. On many occasions they would go with her to appointments, and they gave her as much love and support as they could. After many tests and doctor visits, the doctors and my aunt had decided on a partial lumpectomy, followed by a rigorous regimen of chemo and radiation treatments. Once again my mom was watching someone whom she loved, suffer with this beast! I saw how much this operation scared my mother, how she was constantly worrying. With fear in her eyes, and after many discussions, my mother would repeatedly say to me, "If I ever have this, you will never know." This would anger me so much. It was her famous line that I hated, but she would constantly remind me of it.

Yet, she would encourage my aunt to fight and do everything in her power to beat it. I just didn't understand her rationale. Having started her treatments, my aunt began to struggle with all the side effects. On some of her worst days, my dad would bring her back to my parent's apartment so my mom could cook for her and make sure she was taken care of. I felt helpless and wanted to do as much as I could for her. I helped with the little things like making sure her house was sterile, and made her favorite homemade chicken pot pies. I knew deep down inside she was going to be okay. My aunt was a fighter, much like my grandmother. She showed so much strength, rather than weakness. Yes, she had days when she struggled, but she didn't let them take her down. I am confident in saying she had Grandma's will and determination. I saw her laugh and I saw her cry. I remember a silly hat that my cousin gave her. It had the middle finger embroidered on it, basically saying FU Cancer. I would crack up every time I saw her wear it. (And believe me, she wore it a lot.) She definitely had a sense of humor about it, even though losing her hair was an agonizing thing to go through. She didn't let it stop her. Picking out a pretty wig was just a band-aid, it didn't define who she was. We would constantly remind her that her hair would grow back. I remember she came to my son's Communion and was self-conscious about her wig. I thought she looked beautiful! She really was a warrior in my eyes. I knew this fight was grinding for her, because she was a committed and dedicated worker, this situation didn't allow her to work much. It killed her to sit home and do nothing. She truly loved her job in retail. She was the type of person that was constantly on the go. Time passed and so did treatments, and she slowly began to bounce back. Winning the war against this beast was priceless, and she did just that. She was a true survivor.

I had already decided that I was going to find an oncologist with a close watchful eye, and go under his care. I knew I needed someone in this field besides an OB-GYN to do breast exams and check ups. Some might say this was rash (like my mom), but I knew in my heart it was necessary. I was determined to stay diligent and on top of this. The battle was constant with my mom. She couldn't understand why I was doing this. I told her my reasoning, but she would not agree to do the same. I simply said, "Okay that is your choice, but this is mine." I remember her asking me, "So what would you do if you were to find out you're a high risk person?" and I replied, "I will figure it out when I get to that point." Never mind the fact that I was already told just how high of a risk I was. Keep in mind, doctors were making huge advances at the time in discovering the BRCA gene, and proactive mastectomies were beginning to become more acceptable. I knew I had choices. It seemed far-fetched, and we'd never know if my grandmother had the BRCA gene, but we knew something was definitely brewing in this family. Finding out that my aunt was BRCA negative, still didn't make me feel any less concerned. It was time to research my options.

Through some recommendations, I found a doctor named Alan Kadison. Unknowing and scared, I set up the consult and off I went. (By myself so I could make my own decision.) I honestly didn't want anyone telling me what to do. This was my sole decision. Also, at this time I found myself headed down the road of divorce, so I didn't have much choice but to stand on my own. My mom wasn't going to support something she didn't believe in for herself. My dad knew what I decided and had mixed feelings, but said to do what I felt was right. I felt if I led the way, then maybe, just maybe, my mom would follow. The day of my consultation arrived, and I was a nervous wreck. I called my mom to tell her I was going and she asked once again, "Are you sure you want to do this?" I knew there would be no support from her, but she was in fact curious. Driving myself to the office, I couldn't help wonder . . . *am I being extreme, am I being overcautious*? Some would say yes, but I did what I felt needed to be done. No harm in getting an opinion, right? I had many conversations with myself, talking myself into and talking myself out of it. As I pulled up to the doctor's office, I took a deep breath and spoke to heaven above . . . Grandma. I asked for guidance. I walked through the door, checked in with the front desk and sat nervously in the waiting room. Before I knew it they called my name and sat me down in the doctor's office. In walked a very mild mannered man. He introduced himself as Dr. Alan Kadison. A very soft spoken man, he proceeded to ask me a series of questions. Immediately I felt comfortable with him. Dr. Kadison was thorough, and I liked that. I basically asked him, "Do I belong here, or am I being irrational?" He definitely didn't take my situation lightly, and assured me that I was doing the right thing by taking this initiative. He was concerned about the genetic pattern and the way it was trickling down; it didn't seem to be "skipping generations." He explained the importance of staying on top of my exams and under a doctor's care. He also asked me about my mom and told me how important it was for her to be under a doctor's care as well. I told him about how stubborn she was and how I tried relentlessly to change her mind. Through it all, I found Dr. Kadison to be compassionate, with great bedside manner. At one point in the conversation, he looked at me and said, "If you were my wife or my daughter I would say the same thing to them that I'm telling you." We also discussed the importance of getting tested for the BRCA, the "what if's" if it came back positive, and the choices I would have. This was the first time I heard the words "prophylactic double mastectomy." That definitely shook me, those words were frightening. Yet I knew the extreme measures I may be facing when I walked into the office. After a long conversation, I was taken to another room for an exam and to test for the BRCA gene. "Let's see what the results bring and we'll take it from there," the doctor said. We also set up my first sonogram and mammogram, only to find out I had what are called dense breasts so they really weren't able to see much. "It's like trying to find a snowball in a snowstorm." *Great*, I thought, *so what good are these tests if we can't see anything?* I was always told about the importance of self exams . . . soapy hands in the shower being the best technique. I was told I had cystic breasts, which apparently my mom had as well. I swear I think my mom and I came out of the same mold!

After much anticipation and waiting, the results were in and came back negative. The negative made sense to me, because my aunt was also negative. I didn't expect to be positive. Dr. Kadison was convinced that the cancer was indeed streaming down the line genetically, explaining to me that the BRCA gene is only one factor, and that there were many other mutations that could play a role in breast cancer. He seemed to think early on it was in our DNA. Now, more than ever, I began to realize this was the case. He reminded me again of constant self exams, and to stay on top of my regular check ups. It was difficult to do because some insurance companies didn't want to pay for certain tests. They would try to deny the service due to my young age, even when I had such profound history in the family.

From day one, everything I tried to do seemed to be a challenge. *Why was it so difficult for women to be proactive? Shouldn't they be able to do what they need, in order to beat this?* I just couldn't understand it. It was beyond frustrating. And to be honest, my mom was even more frustrating. Every time I would go for an exam, she would say to me, "It's almost like you're looking for something," and my response was, "It's called being proactive, exactly what you should be doing." She would just ignore me, and say "You know how I feel about that." But I didn't let her persuade me, always hoping that she would one day see the importance and follow my lead. I also had endless conversations with my dad. He told me he tried to talk to her about it as well, but I don't think that even my dad realized the importance of the family DNA. Ironically, my mom would always make sure my aunt stayed on top of her check ups. She constantly reminded her to do so, but never did for herself. This was just mind-blowing. I never understood her way of thinking. I almost gave up on my continued effort with my mom. I carried on with my proactive behavior, never ignoring the importance of staying diligent. I had made up my mind, I would never let this cancer get to me. I promised myself that I would always be one step ahead. As for my mom, I would never give up trying to make her see the importance of taking charge of her health. Unfortunately, cancer hit another woman in my family. This time it was my aunt, who was my dad's sister. This made my mother even more fearful.

Chapter 10

Her Way

It was now the summer of 2013, and I had a suspicion that something was seriously wrong with my mom. She had not been herself for months. She seemed to be tired a lot, she was losing some weight, and my family and I thought she was fighting some sort of depression. At the time, there had been some turmoil in the family, and she wasn't happy. We thought this was playing a role. Normally, on a weekday she would watch my niece, but lately it was draining her. Not being able to pinpoint what was happening, we were all concerned about her health, especially my dad. I was putting a lot of pressure on my mother hoping she would tell me what was wrong. My dad would ask me to back off, believing she was just feeling a little depressed. There were times I would pop in on my lunch break to check in on her and she would be sitting in the apartment, with all the lights off watching T.V. I repeatedly asked her what was wrong, and she would always blow me off saying, "Nothing, I'm fine. I'm just tired." My mother wasn't one to sit still, she was always cooking and cleaning. We used to joke around and call her "Mrs. Clean." She was so clean, in fact, that she would follow the kids around with Windex and wipe fingerprints off the walls and windows. When I noticed her apartment wasn't as immaculate as it had always been, it was a red flag for me. My family and I were truly concerned. Two out of my four brothers lived out of state, so I was constantly in touch keeping them updated. They would call and Facetime her, while she continued to reassure everyone that she was "fine." My son Rocco was 17 and Christian was 13 at the time. They both recognized that their Mima wasn't well. They were very close with my parents and saw them frequently. They immediately sensed something was wrong. That summer my youngest, Christian, decided he was going to spend a lot of time with my mom to help her out. I was working full-time, and couldn't be there during the day, but I would try to run over mid-day. The more time I spent there, the more I realized that something was seriously wrong. I still couldn't put my finger on it. Christian was beginning to notice things more and more as well. He began to tell me some really disturbing stories. One day after I picked him up, he said to me, "Mom, something is really wrong with Mima. You're not listening to me! I heard her, she was in the closet crying, 'I'm dying, I'm dying,'" he said. "What do you mean?" I could feel my heart drop. "Yes, I heard her. I don't know what she was doing in the closet!" By now my suspicions were high. I was very disturbed and couldn't get her to be honest with me. I immediately called my dad, and asked if he knew what this was about. He said he didn't know what was wrong. Again, he thought she was fighting some type of depression. This was what he kept repeating. The fact of the matter was that she wasn't being honest with him either. At the same time that she was battling this so-called depression, she hurt her shoulder. She claimed that she pulled something while lifting up the neighbor's baby. I told her she needed to see the doctor to have it checked. She absolutely refused to go. She was adamant about it, once again, letting her fear of doctors stand in her way. Little did I know there was a consequential reason behind this. I also begged my dad to take her. He said she refused. It was a losing battle, my mom was beyond stubborn. Days passed, and her shoulder began to droop somewhat. She was continuously arguing with my dad over going to the doctor. I felt like I was chasing my tail with her.

I now know she made my dad lie when I asked about a doctor's visit. Instead, they bought a splint for her to wear, saying the doctor had given it to her. Oddly enough, it seemed to have had an effect and she was getting better. I still didn't believe either one of them. They were not fooling me for one minute! Honestly, they weren't fooling any of my brothers either. We all had our suspicions that something was definitely wrong. I knew my mother all too well. I knew her fear of doctors, and I also knew "her way of doing things." Christian continued to go there daily to help her with day-to-day chores. It got so challenging she needed help doing the laundry. He told me that she couldn't even reach down to get the clothes out of the washing machine anymore. My brothers and I were so concerned, we kept approaching our parents, especially my dad, thinking maybe he had some knowledge of what was happening. Yet again, he simply felt that she was fighting some depression, and needed to work through it. He'd say to me, "Sometimes I wake up in the middle of the night, and she is sitting at the edge of the bed crying. When I ask her what's wrong, she says she's just depressed." There was some turmoil in the family at the time, so it would almost make sense. But I wasn't buying it, there was more to it. I began to get angry with my mom and my dad as well. I felt he wasn't handling the situation correctly. There were times I would argue with both of them, and the conversations would get heated to the point that I would walk out. My dad would say to me, "Mind your business, I can handle it." He became as combative as my mom, and it really made me frustrated and angry. In hindsight, my dad was just being protective of my mom. This continued for weeks and months, and I was tired of it. There was nothing my brothers or I could say or do, her mind was made up. She stuck to her "I'm fine" story. Out of concern and exhaustion from the arguing, I began to reach out to my aunt (my mother's sister). I wanted her to know what was happening. I thought maybe she would be able to get through the stubbornness, but my mom would say the same thing to her. I guess she was believable. I felt so frustrated. No one was seeing the need for urgency. *Something was happening here. Why didn't anyone hear me?* With arguments erupting and time passing, all I could do was be diligent in trying to convince her to get checked and constantly keep my eye on her. That was it, my hands were tied. I was beyond angry with her. I spent as much time as I could with my mom, helping with laundry, food shopping, cooking and running any errands.

My mother had lost her eyesight due to a degenerative genetic disease, and could no longer drive. Losing her independence did not make her happy. Normally, she would have come along with me wherever I went, but she wasn't in any condition to run errands. I noticed that she began to lose more weight, enough that it was clearly visible. One day when we were having dinner at my cousin's house, I looked at her from across the table and noticed that one side of her face seemed a little droopy. Looking at her I said, "Mom, why does it look like your face is drooping?" It was difficult to see, she was sitting in direct sunlight, and it was very slight. "What do you mean?" she responded nervously. My aunt had also taken notice of this. But it was so slight, that when she moved away from the sun, it didn't look like much. I found it so strange. My mother blew it off by saying "Yes, it must have been the way the light was hitting my face." I remember thinking, *Could she have had a stroke?* Going home that night, I looked at her face again, and it didn't seem to be too bad. *Was my mind playing tricks on me?* I was so confused, and so desperate for answers. I couldn't believe how stubborn she was and now my dad as well. I felt like I was watching my mother dwindle away with no explanation, other than she was depressed. As time passed, I grew more angry out of sheer frustration, I would yell at my dad, "Don't you see what's happening, or am I the only one who sees this?" "Mind your business, I can take care of her," he would say. "Okay, is that what you want? You want me to stop coming here? You don't want me to help you?" I asked. And that's just what I did. I backed off and gave them their space. There was no other solution, because every time I went there it ended up in an argument. I still checked on her everyday with daily calls, and my brothers did too. We all grew increasingly frustrated. At this point we seemed to hit a brick wall. I can honestly say we all tried our best. There was nothing left to do but sit back and pray for the best. Maybe this was just their generation's way of doing things. Oddly, there were days she seemed to be better, doing her daily chores, and completely throwing me off. I was so confused.

November was here, and she was definitely putting up a good front cooking and doing most of the things she would normally do. By this point, she had lost about 40 pounds or so, yet she seemed to be in better spirits. There were days I would walk into her apartment unannounced, I would find her sitting in the dark, passed out with pillows propping her up, looking tired and sick. One day looking well, another day looking terrible . . . nothing made sense anymore. I began to think she really was depressed. The signs were beginning to make sense. To attempt to bring up a conversation of a doctor's visit was something I wouldn't consider any longer. I couldn't go down that path with her again. Except for this one particular day, I went over to my parents' house to have dinner. I walked into the apartment and happened to notice that things were untidy. My mother, who was the cleanest person I knew (to the point that she was teased for it) had the house in disarray. Slowly walking over to the TV stand, I began to run my finger across the glass, and it was covered with dust. Now, I was certain she was hiding something. This was so out of character. I turned, looked at her and walked over to where she was sitting. She was propped-up with pillows, and my dad was next to her. I bent down, held my finger with the dust on it in front of her and said in a really stern voice, "This isn't like you. I know something is wrong with you, and I am taking you to the doctor, whether you agree or not! Do you hear me?" There was complete silence. My dad didn't say a word either, he just turned and looked at her. There was no way in hell, that by now, he wasn't thinking something was wrong. My mom, just stared at me. Suddenly I heard her mutter the word "Okay." "I'm serious, this has gone on way too long," I said. By now she had a cough that had developed, enough was enough. Once again complying, she simply shook her head yes with an almost blank look on her face. She finally caved. Now, I was sick to my stomach. I knew this wasn't good. How did I know? Because my mother had finally agreed to go see a doctor. That spoke volumes. My mind was racing a mile a minute. While sitting for dinner with my parents, all was pretty silent, and not much was said. We all knew what each other was thinking. After dinner, I immediately called all my brothers to tell them what was going on and what the plan was.

It was now Wednesday, the day before Thanksgiving and I happened to be off from work. Realizing just how serious things were getting, I packed some clothes and went to spend the weekend with my mother. I was able to get a doctor's appointment for Monday morning. I called my mom, told her about the appointment, and that I decided to come to stay with her for the weekend. Strangely, she was okay with it. It was so odd that all of a sudden she was cooperating. I even wondered if she was saying yes to shut me up. But she had a horrible cough, and I figured she wanted to have it checked out. It was getting so bad that I actually asked myself if she might have pneumonia. "Maybe," she said, shrugging me off. Whatever the problem was, it was clear she needed immediate medical attention. Thanksgiving Day had arrived and we headed to dinner at my cousin's house. I called my aunt and my cousin to warn them that my mother wasn't well. I mentioned that I thought something was seriously wrong. I did not want them to be too shocked when they saw her. Arriving at my cousin's, my aunt instantly panicked when she saw how much weight my mom lost. Pulling me aside, she asked me what I thought was wrong. I really had no answer, other than the fact that I thought maybe she had pneumonia. It was so obvious that she wasn't well. I explained that we had an appointment on Monday with a doctor, and my aunt decided it was important that she go with us. She walked over to my mom and said in a stern voice, "I am going with you to the doctor on Monday, I know something is wrong with you!" Again with that blank stare in her eyes, she just nodded her head yes. It was a rough day for all of us pretending to have a nice Thanksgiving, while my mom was obviously very ill. She barely touched any of her favorite foods that day. I was sick to my stomach whenever I looked at her. I was so nervous about what could be happening. Somehow, we got through the day and headed home. It was a very quiet ride, my mother didn't have much to say, and neither did I. My mind was spinning with concern.

That night I grabbed a blanket and a pillow and made myself comfortable on the couch. My parents were sleeping in the next room. They lived in a small apartment. I turned the TV on, my mind racing, and eventually drifted off. I suddenly woke up to a really strange sound. I couldn't figure out what it was, or where it was coming from. I sat up, shut the television off, and just sat there for a minute. *What the hell is that sound?* It was some sort of loud wheezing or gurgling. I got up and tried to follow the sound to determine where it was coming from. It brought me right to my parents' room. Now my stomach was in knots, because I realized it was coming from my mom's side of the bed. I tiptoed over to her, and leaned over to listen to her breathing. *Why is she breathing like that, where is that sound coming from?* I became paralyzed with fear and started shaking. I tried to tiptoe back to the couch without making a sound. I placed the blanket over my mouth to cover the sound of my crying. I was so afraid to learn what could be wrong with her. It was the middle of the night and I couldn't call anyone, I felt helpless. *What the hell is happening?* I kept asking myself. I didn't sleep a wink that night, I couldn't imagine what could possibly be wrong. I tried to convince myself that she must have pneumonia. *What else could it be?* God only knew!

The morning came, I was so nervous I didn't know what to do. My mom had woken and made her way to the bathroom. That's when I grabbed my dad. "Daddy," I said, "did you hear the way that Mommy was breathing last night?" "What do you mean?" he asked, looking totally clueless. I explained what I heard, and he couldn't believe what I was saying. He said that he never heard any sounds like that before. I had to believe him, because my dad was such a deep sleeper nothing would wake him. Now he was as concerned as I was. I called my brothers, my aunt and my cousin to explain what I had witnessed, and reminded them again that I had the appointment for her on Monday. I wanted so badly to ask her if she realized how she was breathing, but I didn't want to upset her. Yet, I felt compelled, "Mom, do you feel okay with that cough? It sounds pretty bad," I said. "What do you mean?" she asked with extreme nervousness. I really didn't want to upset her. "No reason Mom, we're going to the doctor Monday, just try to rest today. I am here to help you." Needless to say the entire day I was holding back the tears. I knew this was deep trouble. She was beginning to look weak and sick. I couldn't wait for the weekend to pass, I wanted it to be Monday already. I spent the entire weekend with my parents helping my mom with whatever she needed. She seemed to be concerned about shopping for Christmas gifts for the grandchildren, so we made a list and I headed out to shop. I hung by her side all weekend. I cleaned the apartment, did some cooking and laundry. Somehow, I convinced her to let me put up some Christmas lights. Mom always loved Christmas. It was her favorite time of the year, but not this year for some reason. As the weekend slipped by she seemed to be getting weaker and she was sleeping a lot. It was strange that she would watch TV and constantly drift in and out. She had no energy. At one point I mentioned that I thought we should go to the emergency room and she flipped out on me. She insisted we wait for Monday. I had no choice but to comply. Finally, it was Sunday night. My dad was in the living room, and my mom and I were lying on her bed just snuggling up to watch her favorite movie, *Mamma Mia*. I was never too old to lie on the bed and snuggle with my mom. This was something we always did together. I loved her so much. She truly was my best friend and extremely special to me. I realized that something serious was happening, all I wanted to do was be close to her. While we watched the movie she would drift in and out, which I found odd. "Mom, are you sleeping?" I would ask. She didn't answer. She just seemed so lethargic. Then all of a sudden I heard that same wheezing and gurgling sound. "Mom, wake up," I panicked, "are you sleeping?" I was getting nervous. "What's wrong?" she said, as she woke up, in a lifeless, sluggish voice. "Did you not hear the way you're breathing?" I asked. "No, what do you mean?" she nervously asked. Seeing the panic on her face I didn't want to upset her more. "Never mind, we're going to the doctor tomorrow just relax," I said. My heart was racing. I didn't know what to think when I heard those noises coming from her. I put my arms around her. I could feel her holding me. I felt my eyes begin to fill with tears and I didn't want to cry. Lying there for a bit, it started to get late. I decided I was going to stay the night again, but my mom insisted that I go home and get the boys ready for school the next day. Reluctantly, I agreed to leave. I also wanted to go home and make some calls that I couldn't make with her around. The plan was that I would come pick her up the next morning, because my dad had to go to work. I also knew that my aunt was going to meet me at the doctor's office, not realizing the severity of what was to come. I headed home, got the boys ready and made sure things were in order. I was so worried, I called my brothers and my aunt to tell them everything that was going on. I also called Fran and begged her to meet me at the doctor's office. Fran of course agreed. As it turned out my mother had already called her and asked her to come along. I didn't find that odd, because after all, they were best friends. My mom always turned to Fran for medical advice. She trusted her immensely. That night I didn't get a drop of sleep, my mind was racing like a hamster wheel. I just kept begging God to please let her be okay. I knew one thing for sure, I didn't want to lose her.

Monday morning came and the boys went off to school. I was riddled with anxiety that morning and could not wait to get to my mom's house. When I arrived, I found her oddly calm. My dad was heading off to work, he walked over and kissed her goodbye. It was then that my mom looked at me and said, "Can you do my make-up for me and fix my hair?" "Sure Mom. You know it's going to be okay," I said. She just looked at me and shook her head from side to side, as if she knew it wasn't going to be. "Are you sure you don't need me to come?" my dad asked. "Fran is meeting us there, I will call you if we need you," I said. With some hesitation, he headed off to work. "How do you feel today, Mom?" I asked. "Not too good," she replied. "It's okay, we are going to figure this out today." I said. I walked over and put my arms around her and hugged her so tight, not wanting to let go. My eyes were welling up and so were hers. "Come on, let's do your hair and make-up," I said. *Was it that she was too weak to do her own make-up and hair, or was this a moment she wanted to share with me?* As I did her make-up I reminded her of how beautiful I thought her skin was, and asked her why she never thought herself to be pretty? When she was young she was elegant and classy, something I admired. "I always thought my sister was prettier than me," she chuckled. My mom always seemed to lack confidence. She was truly a beautiful woman, especially in my eyes. I got her ready and it was time to go. My stomach was doing flips, but I knew it was time to find out what the hell was going on. We hopped in the car, and all of a sudden she began to stress over me mailing an envelope. "Joanne, listen to me. It's really important that when you get back you mail the envelope I left on the counter," she said. Not saying it once, but a few times. "Okay, okay," I said at that moment. It was the last thing I was thinking about. A stupid piece of mail, and why was she even saying when "you" get back? She didn't say when "we" get back. I found that to be strange, but didn't put too much thought into it. As we pulled up to the doctor's office, I saw Fran and my two aunts standing outside. I stopped for a minute and thought to myself, *why is my other aunt here as well?* "Mom, all three of them are here, why?" I asked. She looked at me and said, "I called them because I wanted them all to be here." *Okay,* I thought. She was so fearful of doctors, it didn't surprise me. We got out of the car, and to be honest they all looked like gloom and doom to me. What was I missing here?

We walked into the waiting room and got her checked in. It was a very small office. We were sitting close together without uttering a word. I began to think to myself, *what's going on here? Why the sad faces?* My mom seemed oddly calm. At this point, I became suspicious and kept wondering what she was hiding from me. "MaryJean," the nurse called. I got up to go in with her, and she turned and said, "I want Fran to come in also." The three of us headed into the examination room. I was still totally clueless. The nurse asked us to step out of the room so my mom could change into her gown. Fran and I stood outside the door. Fran really wasn't saying much. They called us back in, then the doctor came in and introduced himself. He proceeded to ask my mom what brought her in today. There was silence, so I said, "My mom has this terrible cough, she's breathing funky and I think she may have pneumonia." "Okay, anything else?" he asked. Mom sat quietly. Then, Fran looked at her, stared and said, "MaryJean, go ahead, tell the doctor what you told me on the phone last night." *Wait, what?* I could feel my heart beginning to pound through my chest. Mom just sat there. "Tell him about the lump on your neck," Fran said. "Yes, I have a lump on my neck," she said. The doctor just looked at her as if he was waiting for more. "Tell him about the breast," Fran said. "HOLD ON! What's going on here?" I said. I began to panic. Fran was trying to keep me calm. My insides began to shake. "Mom, why didn't you tell me this? What is going on?" I was furious. The doctor began to examine her neck. I saw the lump, and began to lose it. "Mrs. Ameruoso, you have to tell me everything. It's important. How long did you know you had these lumps?" the doctor asked. "Quite a while," she said. "Mom, what do you mean? Why wouldn't you tell anyone? Does Daddy even know?" "No, I didn't tell anyone," she said calmly, as if she were numb. "May I take a look at the breast?" the doctor asked. She just shook her head yes and sat there as he pulled open the gown, I immediately peeked over his shoulder and suddenly felt my legs begin to shake. I wanted to vomit. I could not believe what I was seeing. I had never, in my life, seen anything like this. Her breast was rotting from the inside out. My entire body went numb. All I knew was panic and anger. I couldn't hide how upset I was with her. I kept saying, "Why, why did you do this?" It didn't matter how many times I asked, she just sat there with no words, which made me more angry. What could she possibly have said to me that would make sense of what she had done? The doctor saw my reaction and realized that I was as dumbfounded as he was. "You didn't know about this?" he asked. "Of course I didn't, would I be freaking out like this?" I said. The doctor then asked Fran and I to leave the room so he could do a full examination and speak privately with my mom. Walking out of the exam room, I turned to Fran. "Please tell me what the hell is going on," I cried. "Your mother called me and her sister last night. She told us that she knew she had breast cancer. She found the lump months ago in her breast," she said. "Why wouldn't she tell us?" I asked. "Was she that afraid of going to see the doctor?" I ran into the waiting room in hysteria to grab my aunt and see what she knew. Apparently my mom called her sister the night before to warn her about what we were going to find out. She told her that she knew she had breast cancer, it was far gone and that not even my father knew about it. I could not process what I was hearing, it was like time was standing still. It felt surreal, as if everything was moving around me. I had no idea what was happening. Heading back to the room, I remained outside the door talking to myself, repeating the words "Why, why would she do this!" But deep down inside I knew why. This was her biggest fear . . . breast cancer. And I knew my mom's way of thinking. I recalled the words at that moment, "If I ever have breast cancer, you're never going to know it." She had spoken this message to me many times. *Well, she wasn't joking about that, was she?* I was so damn angry! *How dare she do this! Not only to herself, but to her entire family! To the people that loved her so much and that would have done anything for her. How was I even going to tell my dad? Oh my God. My dad! How could he have not known this? What the hell do I do now?* As I waited outside the door, with all of this racing through my mind, the doctor came out and said, "I need to speak to you." He faced me and placed both hands on my shoulders. He spoke in a very calm voice and he said the words no one ever wants to hear. "Your mother has stage four breast cancer, and doesn't have much time left. She's very sick." Honestly, by the look of her breast I knew it was bad, but I wasn't ready to believe it. Pushing his hand off my shoulders I screamed, "You don't know what you're fucking talking about! You haven't even done an X-ray! How could you know this?" "I'm telling you this isn't good. This is stage four and it's all over her body," he said calmly. "Her lungs are filled with fluid, and she may have only days to live. We have to get her over to radiology to do X-rays stat." "No, no, no, stop talking like this, I am taking her out of here!" I yelled. I was hysterical. At this point everyone was trying to keep me calm. "I have to call my Dad," I cried as I ran out the door. I didn't have the heart to tell him the truth over the phone, but it was the quickest way of getting the news to him. I had to pull myself together. When I called, my brother answered the phone. "Hello?" I began to cry. "Jo, what's wrong?" he asked. "I am at the doctor with Mommy. He is telling me that she has stage four breast cancer and is very sick! I need to speak to Daddy, right now. But you cannot tell him, I'll tell him when he meets us." As I was explaining this to my brother, my dad overheard him getting upset and grabbed the phone out of his hands. "What's wrong?" he shouted. "Daddy, you have to meet us. Mom has to get X-rays, she has fluid in her lungs and she needs to get some tests done," I said. "What's going on?" he asked again. "I'm not really sure," I said. "Just meet us at the x-ray facility, and I will talk to you when you get there." I immediately hung up the phone and ran back into the office. They were moving quickly. The doctor had all her scripts ready to go. Barging through the examination room, I was so angry and full of emotion. I wanted answers. "Mommy, why, just tell me why you did this? You know I would have been there for you every step of the way. Why were you so afraid?" I cried. My emotions were raging. I didn't know what to say, do, or feel. I was just angry. She began to cry. "I didn't want to be a burden to anyone," she said. "What do you mean, a burden? That's ridiculous! I am your daughter, I would have done anything for you, and you know that," I cried. That may have been what she was telling me and herself, but I knew it was deep fear that gripped her. I looked at her and said, "You almost lived up to your words didn't you? Like you always said, if you ever have breast cancer, I would never know it." She then looked at me very sternly and said, "This is going to go down my way." I was irate at this point, yet crumbling inside for her pain. Could you imagine realizing that you have breast cancer, and not telling anyone? Not having a single soul to lean on? I think this is what was killing me. The thought that she had walked through this all alone was so profoundly upsetting. I tried to make her see the importance of preventative care. I fought the endless battle of trying to make her proactive. I constantly tried to convince her to stand up to this beast that was lurking in our family. It all made me furious! I was angry not only with her, but with God. It wasn't fair. My faith was shaken to its core. I kept thinking *why God, tell me why?* Walking her to the car, I was so infuriated I struggled to keep control. We got in the car and I was crying, I couldn't hold myself back. "Why Mom, tell me why? Do you even realize how bad this is?" She didn't answer me. All she said was to make sure I mailed the envelope. Really, right now she was so worried about the damn envelope. That wasn't a concern for me at all, a stupid piece of mail. "Did you call your father?" she asked me. "Yes, but I didn't have the heart to tell him over the phone," I said. "No, I will tell him," she said. Arriving for the X-rays, we pulled up and my dad was there along with my aunts and Fran. Once again, before stepping out of the car, she sternly reminded me that this was going to go down her way. There would be no MRI's and no treatments. There would be no questioning it. "You understand me?" she asked. I couldn't help myself and asked, "Mom, haven't you already done it your way? Believe me, how could I ever forget your words." She just looked at me and said "I am so sorry." At this point I didn't know what to say. Getting out of the car she walked over to my dad. I stayed back, as I watched my father and mother speak. I knew that she had told him when I saw my dad put his arms around her, crying uncontrollably. He was holding her tight. Mom stood there almost expressionless with her arms by her side. Who was she trying to be brave for? Why wasn't she showing emotion? I couldn't make sense of anything at all. I walked over to them and told my dad to take her in because I had to make some calls.

As they walked into the building she remained weirdly calm, with that blank stare I had seen before. Now, I had to make the dreaded phone calls to my other brothers, who had already gotten word of what was happening. My phone was ringing off the hook. We were all in shock. Everyone kept asking, what do you mean? *How could this happen? I had no answers, none of us did. We all felt so helpless and dumbfounded. How could we have been so blind to the signs? How could we lose our mother, the most precious person to us? What about all the grandkids? She was their world! This cannot be happening,* I thought. She was our protector, the glue of the family, the one we could always turn to. This was one of the worst days of our lives. Everyone wanted a minute by minute update, and yet I had no answers. Who knew what the hell was happening, it was all evolving so quickly, yet it felt strangely slow. I was still begging God, "please let this not be true." X-rays were taken, and it was decided that my mom needed to immediately head to the hospital to drain the fluid from her lungs. Now it all started to make sense, that gurgling wheeze I would hear when she slept had a cause. We also needed to speak to the oncologist as soon as possible, so that she could better explain things to us. My dad took my mom in his car as we all headed to the hospital. The same exact hospital where my grandmother passed away. I couldn't even imagine what was going through her mind. Was she thinking she was going to die the same way her mother did, and in the same hospital? Remember, she had a fear of hospitals and doctors, yet in the midst of this chaos, she calmly reminded us that this was going to be done "her way." I was so sick and tired of hearing those fucking words. *Just stop it,* I thought. I was trying to console my dad, neither one of us could wrap our heads around why she would do this. "Daddy, are you telling me that you had no idea that this was happening?" I asked. "None, nothing! She never led onto anything, I just thought she was depressed," he said. I remember putting my arms around him to console him, he was beside himself. I was trying to convince him and myself that it was going to be okay. How naive of me. The doctors were already telling us how grim the reality was. Maybe we were just refusing to acknowledge it. We were grasping at hope. Can you blame us? Do you know when something just feels surreal? This was one of those moments, when you want to close your eyes and make it all disappear.

Mom was now settled in the emergency room, and my aunt and I were in the room with her. At one point, my aunt asked her the same question . . . why? We could ask as many times as we wanted, but the fact was that it was too late to go back and try to fix this. Besides, she never had an answer. Nor did she have to give one, I knew her reasoning. Not that it made any sense, I just knew my mom's way of thinking. As she lay in the bed, she looked at her sister and said to her, "I don't want to die, I want to go see the Christmas tree in the city one more time." My aunt looked at her and said, "You're not going to die. And we will take you to see the tree, I promise." God only knows how much we all wanted to believe that this would be true, but it wasn't up to us. By now we had met with the oncologist, which happened to be someone I had previously worked for. She had many questions for us. My dad was so overwhelmed and emotional, that he wasn't handling this well. He said to the doctor, "This is my daughter. I give you full permission to speak with her." He was just so distraught, he couldn't even think. My aunt and my dad stayed in the room with my mom, while I walked into the hallway to speak with the doctor. She began by asking me how long ago my mom had found the lump in her breast. Honestly, I had no clue, not even my dad knew. Apparently, we were all left in the dark. The oncologist was astonished by our lack of knowledge, trying to imagine how my mom could have possibly kept this to herself. "Why would she do this?" she asked me. I was as frustrated as the doctor. I had no answers for her. The doctor informed me that she asked my mom, but couldn't seem to get a straight answer from her. "I believe your mother has had this cancer for at least a year or so, judging by the test we ran. It seems to have been a slow-moving cancer. If she would have gone to a doctor as soon as she found the lump, this would be a whole different scenario," she explained. "So what do we do now?" I asked. "We will drain some fluid tomorrow to make her comfortable, and see how well that goes," she said. Not giving us any plans for treatments, or seeming to give us any hope, I asked her, "What's the plan moving forward?" "Joanne, there is no plan. I am sorry to say, this is terminal. All we can do is keep her comfortable." she said. At that moment I felt like the blood was draining from my body. I just stood there looking at the doctor, truly speechless. I was desperate for hope and so damn angry. Grasping for anything I wanted to hear, I asked her, "Why can't you do a mastectomy and treatment? There has to be something you can do!" "I am so sorry Joanne, this is past the point of help," the doctor said. "Again, we will do all we can to make sure she is comfortable." Have you ever held so much grief in your heart that you felt like you just couldn't breathe? That was how I felt. I couldn't speak. It felt like my heart was shattering to pieces. All I wanted to do was fix this. *Please God help me fix this!* I felt so small and helpless against this beast, this cancer, that seemed to have no mercy on the women in my family. How would I explain this to my dad or anyone else? This was unraveling so quickly, I couldn't even process it. I was so angry, I had to know the truth. I stormed back into the room and asked again. "Mom, just how long ago did you discover this lump, please be honest with me!" "Maybe six months or so, I don't know," she said. "It's more than six months and you know it!" I said furiously. "The doctor said that this was a slow moving cancer, so tell me the truth!"

She picked her head up, looked at me and my aunt and then said, "Like a year or more." My aunt and I just looked at her. She knew what we were thinking. How did she expect us to react to this? She was afraid to tell us the truth because she knew we would be upset with her. My aunt and I were crying, as she looked to us once again reminding us that this was going to be done her way now. "Yes Mom." I said defeated. "We know you are doing this your way. You have said it loud and clear to all of us!" I had this nauseating feeling in my stomach, again asking myself *why would she do this?* Having to inform my brothers about her terminal cancer and what was going on absolutely devastated me. It was the hardest hit we have ever felt. Our mom was our entire world, and she was dying. None of us could save her, we were simply helpless. At the mercy of God now, all we could do was pray. She wasn't just any Mom . . . she was special. Not just to us, but to so many who adored and loved her. We were all about to lose an amazing wife, mother, grandmother, sister, aunt, and friend. In a blink of an eye life was about to change forever, and we could not control it.

It was Tuesday morning, and it was time for the fluid extraction procedure. My dad and I were at the hospital. Still in shock, we tried to be positive around my mom. I knew that she knew there was no hope left. I believe she was accepting of her decision and was somehow coming to peace with it in her own way. For some reason she would always have this expressionless, blank look on her face. The doctor came into the room and explained what they would be doing and how long the procedure would take. Then they rolled her off to the OR. I kept praying asking God for a miracle. The procedure went by quickly, and she was wheeled right back into her room. She seemed to look better and was even breathing easier. Her face seemed to have regained some color. We all were a little relieved when we saw her looking more alert. "How do you feel Mom?" I asked. "Much better right now," she said. "That makes me happy, and tomorrow they will do the other lung and you'll get some more relief," I said. I was still so angry, but all I could think about was how she could beat this. My dad, I think, was still in such shock he didn't know what questions to ask the doctors. Were we all that clueless, or was it that we just wanted to believe in the optimistic possibilities? Where was the hope? What were we even praying for? Maybe there would be a miracle. After all, we do believe in miracles! Why not one for my Mom? Shockingly, she began to feel a little bit better and even developed an appetite. She was talking to us, and joking around a little bit with my dad. Even though my dad was beside himself, he wanted to make her smile. My brothers who lived out of state were Facetiming her and calling her constantly. As her grandchildren, family and friends gathered around, I couldn't help but think this is how it was when Grandma passed away. And that was something I was not willing to accept, at least not right now. I was in complete denial. Refusing to bring myself to that place in time. We were going to fight this. I was telling myself this wasn't final!

The doctors were coming in and out, still questioning how long she knew about these lumps. I of course had to ask one more time, "Mom, please tell me how long did you know about this?" She sat speechless for a moment then she looked at me and said, "I told you, about a year." "Mom really, the truth please," I said firmly. "Over a year?" I asked. She finally replied honestly, "Yes, about a year or more." It was so hard to swallow, that she hid it for so long. It made NO sense to me . . . ZERO! "So you're telling me that you knew for so long, and you didn't think for one second you should tell anyone, not even Daddy,"

I was so distressed. "I told you," she said, "I didn't want to be a burden to anyone." I really had to control my anger at this point, because I knew that what she had said was far from the truth. Burden? That was nothing more than an excuse. She had so many people, including myself, that would have walked to the ends of the earth for her. I knew my mother better than anyone else. I knew it was her fear that held her back! Fear of doctors, fear of hospitals, fear of breast cancer, fear of it all! I imagined the fear that she must have had when she discovered the lump. So fearful that she, along with the lump, hid far from the truth. This was not something you could just ignore and wish away. It was senseless to be annoyed at her any longer. She began to cry, and so did I. Was I crying out of resentfulness, or was I feeling so sad that she actually felt she would have been a burden to us? Didn't she know how much we loved her and would do anything for her? And I mean ANYTHING! I loved my mother fiercely. There were not enough words to describe how incredibly special she was to me. She was irreplaceable and invaluable to my family and me. It hurt me to think she truly felt this way. With nothing left to say, I walked over to her, put my arms around her and told her how much I loved her. "I just wish I had known Mom, the doctor said this was a slow moving cancer. It didn't have to be this way," I was sobbing as I spoke these words and held her tightly. "You have to respect my decision," she said as she cried. I didn't know what else to say or do. She then reminded me of her other motto in life . . . when the body is ready to go, we go! I was WAY too outraged to accept this right now. There was no way she could rationalize this with me. Maybe I was being too harsh with her, but I just couldn't shift my emotions. My anger and bitterness was taking over. Can you blame me? I relived the endless conversations and arguments of trying to get her to be proactive . . . I mean endless, what good did it do? She and I were on opposite ends of the spectrum when it came to breast cancer.

Oddly, Mom never asked what the doctors were saying. It was as if she already knew. I now understand why she finally agreed to go to the doctor. She knew it was time. She was done hiding and battling this disease alone. With this state of mind, Mom began to remind us of her wishes. NEVER put her on life support . . . EVER! This was one thing she was always adamant about. But who the hell wanted to have this conversation right now? I told her, don't remind me, I already know this! Besides, I was still in denial looking for a small miracle. I was grasping for any drop of hope! Still in shock, the word was spreading quickly through family and friends. My phone was ringing non-stop. While telling people the grim news, I stayed in my little world of hope. I really had no answers for anyone. In my mind this wasn't over, we were going to fight this to the very end! My family and I were still in disbelief and didn't know how to process this. All my dad knew was that he was losing his high school sweetheart, the woman he built his life with, the woman he had five children with . . . how could he ever make it through without her? My heart was just broken for him. Mom seemed to be in better spirits with her family surrounding her. Her grandchildren were her light and joy! They actually brought some smiles to her face that night. And they were also relieved to see her feeling and looking better. By this time, the doctors had come in and said they would try to drain the fluid out of the other lung on Thursday. That would help and give her some more relief. They also began to have the conversation with us about how they would keep her "comfortable" when the time came. *What the hell are they even saying?* I thought. *Keep her comfortable?* I wanted to know what the next steps were, never mind keeping her comfortable! I just wanted them to stop throwing that word around. Comfortable to me meant final. I couldn't even process what had transpired in these past few days, never mind talk about her final days. *Please just make it stop*, I thought. I left the hospital that night knowing my mom had some relief, I was now setting my sights on tomorrow's plan. I had to go and get some rest, I needed to work the next day. My boys and I kissed her goodbye, while I reminded her how much we loved her. We headed home. It had been a long two days.

Wednesday morning was a work day. My plan was to get the boys off to school and then shoot over to the hospital to quickly pay her a visit. I was just about to walk out the door, when my phone rang. It was my mom. "Mom?" "Hi," she said. "You okay, how do you feel?" I asked. "Yes, actually I feel so much better this morning," she said. For a minute there I could feel a small stream of happiness go through my body. "Okay, well I can't even tell you how happy that makes me! I was just leaving to go see you. Do you want me to bring you anything?" I asked. "Actually I do," she said. "Can you bring me my favorite egg sandwich and can you stop by the apartment and grab my rosary beads from my room?" This totally came out of left field, she sounded so good! "Of course," I said, "Give me some time, I'll be there as soon as I can." I hung up the phone in a hurry, so that I could grab her and my dad's breakfast, and of course get her rosary beads. I was so happy to hear her voice and, more so, to hear that she had an appetite. This was a small glimmer of hope that I was holding on to. I arrived at the hospital, with a flicker of happiness, glad to find her sitting up smiling and actually looking good. My dad looked like he was relieved as well. "Doesn't she look better?" he asked. "Yes, you really do Mom.

Your color looks great." I said. I wanted to cry tears of joy as she smiled when I handed her the rosary beads. I knew how important The Holy Rosary was to her. My mom was devoted to the Blessed Mother and always prayed the Hail Mary. She turned and said to me, "I really feel better since they drained the fluid." "Well, I'm happy that you also have an appetite. Here, eat your sandwich," I said. I handed it to her and she just smiled at me. Boy, she wasn't kidding, she was in the mood for it . . . she ate the whole thing! This was the most I had seen her eat in months. I was ecstatic at this moment. My brother walked in and also couldn't believe how well she looked. We were all so overjoyed. I couldn't stay long and really wanted to see the doctor before I headed to work, but I couldn't wait any longer. Besides, the plan was set. The doctors were going to drain her other lung the next day, which was Thursday. Trying to understanding and accept the severity of this cancer, is what my family and I were doing, yet always holding on to any string of hope. Why would I throw in the towel and just let this beast take her? Praying for a miracle was an option in my world. I was going to leave this up to God. I had to leave it in his hands and put my trust in him. Of course God knew I didn't want to lose her. I wasn't ready, not that we would ever be ready to lose a parent. I kept asking God to "fix it." Walking over, I kissed my mom goodbye, and reassured her that it was going to be okay. It was time for me to go to work. "Love you Mom," I said. "I'll call and check on you. I'll bring you some dinner later." "Love you too," she said with a smile. I headed off to work, trying to stay focused and to go about my day. My dad stayed with her, keeping in contact with me throughout the day. He never left her side. The work day went by pretty quickly. The boys and I grabbed some food and went to visit Mom. We found her perky and looking pretty good. She had nice color in her face and she was a little more talkative. My boys just adored their grandmother, both my parents for that matter. They were her pride and joy. Everyone was visiting and keeping her spirits up. All the grandchildren were there and you could see that made her mood bright. My dad ran home quickly to shower, while family and friends were in and out visiting. I wished for time to stand still. *What next?* I would think. *Was there even a next? Or do we just wait?* Sitting at the edge of her bed, I looked at her. She knew what I was thinking. It was the same damn question I never seemed to get the answer to . . . WHY? Of course I would ask her again. And she would respond with, "We are doing this my way." *Yeah* okay, I thought, just blowing those ridiculous words right off. If you asked me, we were going to battle this and win! Now I can see just how naive I was.

The night came and went, and so did people. It was time for us to go home. As much as I didn't want to, I knew the boys had school and I had to work. I was comfortable with the fact that my dad never left her side, so she was never alone. I headed out with the boys, with the game plan that was set for tomorrow. I reminded her that she would feel even better tomorrow when they drained the fluid out of the other lung. I kissed and hugged her goodnight, told her how much we loved her . . . I didn't know this would be the last time I would hear her say the words "I love you too, JoJo." The boys and I headed home to try to relax a little bit and get ready for the next day. I remember that night lying in my bed crying and praying. I talked to my grandmother, asking her to help us. I begged God and all the angels to help, and please send down a miracle. I could not imagine life here on earth without her. *Please God don't take her from us, especially from my Dad.* She was his entire world. They were together fifty five plus years, that's like losing half your soul. My mom was a young seventy three. I would never have believed we could lose her at this age. Eventually, I drifted off from sheer exhaustion to be woken by the most dreaded phone call . . . it was my dad, crying in hysteria. "Joanne, you have to call your brothers and come here right now!" "What do you mean, what's wrong?" I cried. It felt like my heart left my body, I couldn't breathe. "Mommy took a turn for the worse, and we need to make a decision," he was sobbing. "What, oh my God! What do you mean make a decision?" I screamed. "Just get here quick!" he cried. "I am coming right now!" I frantically ran to the boys room, got the boys up, got into the car and flew over to the hospital! I called all of my brothers, my aunt and cousin to tell them to get to the hospital as soon as possible! I didn't understand, what had just happened? I kept thinking, *she was fine when we left her! She was eating, she was alert and smiling. Oh my God what went wrong?* I was panic stricken and begging, *please God don't let this happen! Please Mom fight, don't give up, Grandma PLEASE, don't take her, we need her here! PLEASE somebody help her!!!* We arrived at the hospital, and ran down the hallway. I saw my Dad. He was distraught. He could barely speak. "Daddy what happened, I don't understand? When I left she was doing better," I cried. "I don't know, she started to labor in her breathing. The doctors came in and said her lungs were filling up and she is basically drowning in her own fluids. They said there is nothing else they can do, except make her comfortable now." He could barely get these words out. "Make a decision?" I asked. "Why can't they drain the fluids again, why not, I just don't understand!" My brothers and I were beside ourselves. *This cannot be happening, somebody please do something* I kept crying in my head. At this point the doctors had come down and explained everything to my brothers and me. They expressed how sorry they were. There was nothing left to do except make her comfortable. She would be sedated enough that she would just drift away. *What is happening* I thought? *We just found out only four days ago that she had stage four breast cancer, and we didn't even get a chance to fight it!* I kept thinking *how unfair this was. No way, give us a shot! It was like we were living this bad dream. Was this really happening?* The doctors needed a signature for the DNR, she did not want life support, or resuscitation. I did not know how my dad was standing, because all I felt was a weakness in my knees. I was numb. I wanted to buckle. We had to discuss this. As a family we all knew my mom's wishes. She had made it very clear in her lifetime, we were to never think about putting her on life support. We all agreed and my dad had to do the most difficult thing of his life . . . sign the consent papers for the DNR. The reality had finally hit me . . . my beautiful mother was facing the end of her life. I was losing one of the most precious people in my world.

Phone calls were made and family and friends gathered around to say their goodbyes. The priest came to give my mom her last rights and final blessings. She continued to clench the rosary in her hands. Mom never let go of them. In my head I kept repeating, *Why mom, why?* As I held her hand, all I could do was cry. I never felt the weight of so much pain, a weight that my body couldn't endure. How would my dad survive this, if my brothers and I couldn't? All of this didn't make any sense, and probably never would. Could I ever justify her actions, or respect her decision like she asked me to? No, not when I knew that this could have been avoided, with a simple annual checkup. My mom had chosen her own destiny by sealing her own fate. I didn't have to agree with it though. All the endless arguing I did with her to go for check-ups, be proactive, it didn't matter anymore. She was doing it "her way!" like she always said she would. As I knelt down by her bedside, still praying for a miracle, there was a pivotal moment. A moment when I realized, there was no more hope, and there was no miracle! Once I began to acknowledge this, I began to pray and ask God to take her peacefully. I couldn't bear to watch her suffer for days, that would be completely selfish of me. No one should ever have to suffer, ever! I kept whispering in my Mom's ear that it was okay. It was okay to rest now. I promised her that I would take care of my dad, and kept whispering . . . "I love you Mom, I love you so much it hurts!" She was my world, my everything, my rock, my confidant, my best friend . . . she was my Mother. Her breathing began to labor, we knew that time was running out. The doctors continued to keep her comfortable, making sure she would feel no pain, as they were coming in and out checking on her vitals. There were times we would hear my mom mumbling words, and we tried to figure out what exactly she was saying. It wasn't in fact a mumble. As my mom clutched onto her rosary beads, she was praying the Hail Mary. When my dad realized she was praying, he put his hands over hers, filled with so much grief, and prayed with her. Time was passing us by, and every minute felt like an hour as we waited for her to take her last and final breath. I walked over to my father and said "Dad, she needs to hear it from you. You have to tell her it's okay to go." I was always a believer in this. When my grandmother died, I made sure I spoke those words to her. So my dad did just that. I am sure those were the most difficult words he ever uttered. Hearing him say to her, "Go ahead my sweetheart, it's okay to go," was heart wrenching! Shortly after, things began to change and her breathing became more shallow with every minute. There were moments we thought she had left us, and then suddenly . . . another breath. I knew I had to tell her again that it was okay to go. Whispering in her ear, I said, "Go Mommy, go be at peace, we all love you. I love you more than you will ever know. I would have done anything for you! I promise I will take care of Daddy." She was surrounded by nothing but love . . . her beautiful husband, children, sister, grandchildren, great grandchildren, nieces, nephews, and her best friends. We all stood, cried and prayed. These were the people who loved her the most. Without warning we witnessed the most precious person in our world take her last deep breath, as she crossed over to Heaven. Her eyes were closed, and peacefully my beautiful mother drifted away. Her soul left her body, flew high above the heavens and reunited with her loved ones. I could feel my body collapse with grief, shaking inside, sobbing to the point of breathlessness . . . this is the day I was left with a void in my heart forever! December 5, 2013 my beautiful, courageous mother was given her wings. This was also the day that my mom's FEAR became my FIGHT! In shock over what had occurred in just four short days, life was forever changed as we knew it. My entire family was completely devastated. Walking my father down the hospital hallway, while he left my mom behind in that cold and lonely room, were the most difficult steps we had to take. All I wanted to do was run back to the room and wake her! I wanted to scream and shake her until she would breathe again!! I wanted someone to wake ME and tell ME this was all a bad dream! As much as I wanted to do that, I knew I couldn't. I had to be strong for my dad. He became so fragile, I had never seen him like this. Rarely did I ever see him cry. He had always been a pillar of strength for us all, and now we had to be strong for him. Holding his arm as we left the hospital, I could feel him shaking. He was crying, "I'm all alone now!" I needed to let him know that he was NEVER going to be alone. Trying to stay strong for him, I turned to him and said, "Daddy I promise you, I will take care of you. Me and the boys will always be here . . . you will never be alone!" My heart was aching for him. I was sustaining his pain, along with my own. My dad was certainly in no position to drive home by himself. I sent my youngest, Christian, to go with him.

Walking to my car, I felt so alone and scared. I sat in my car with nothing left to do but cry. I cried so hard, that I was breathless. I couldn't contain myself or get it together. I knew I wasn't capable of driving. I kept praying to all the angels above, all the loved ones that I lost, asking them "Where are you? Where are you all when I need you most?" You see, I have always been a faithful person, one who believes in mediums, and the signs from our loved ones who have passed. Now, while I clenched my steering wheel with both hands and rested my forehead on the wheel, suddenly this calm ran through my body. Feeling compelled, I looked up and there it was! I was looking at a light box, with the numbers 521! This number was so significant in my life. It represented the day that Dino passed away (5/21) and it represented my grandmother's birthday (2/2/15). I was at first baffled by this, thinking *why am I seeing this?* And then it hit me. Today's date was in fact 12/5 . . . 521 backwards! This was for sure a sign. The heavens above were telling me, she was okay. Now I knew that I was not alone, because this beautiful sign had just been sent. I needed to pull myself together and get home to my dad's.

I arrived at my dad's safely. We were all exhausted. My family and I were with him along with his grandchildren. He needed us now more than ever. I think I was mourning more for my dad, than for myself. I heard him in the bathroom, he was crying and speaking to my mom. It was so pitiful to listen to. He was saying . . . "You left me, why did you have to leave me. What am I going to do without you?" He was so emotionally frail, I knew I couldn't possibly leave him alone that night. Even though my brother and his family lived upstairs, I didn't want him to be by himself. My dad needed all of us, now more than ever. After having a bite to eat, my boys and I decided we would stay the night. We opened up the sofa bed and crawled in out of sheer exhaustion. The boys fell asleep. I couldn't seem to rest my mind. I tried, but I laid there with my mind racing. Though my eyes were closed, I could feel the tears streaming down my cheeks. My heart physically hurt! I had never felt pain like this before. It was as if I had needles in my chest. Lying there crying to my Mom, I told her how much I was hurting, and that I needed her. Unfamiliar with this void in my heart, one that I knew could never be filled again, I was feeling hollow and empty. I could only imagine how my father was feeling. I found myself constantly talking and praying to my mother. Suddenly I felt this calm come over my body. And just like that, the most incredible vision appeared. It was my beautiful mother. It was as if I was looking at a picture of her with burnt edges around it. She was young and so beautiful. In the vision I was seeing, she was bending down kissing a little girl on the nose! For a second I didn't know who it was, then I quickly realized that the little girl was me! My tears slowly began to fade. I can't explain the calm that streamed through my body. It was the most beautiful thing I had ever encountered in my life. I couldn't hear any sounds around me. There was pure silence and peace throughout my body. I was now convinced that my mom had just visited me spiritually. I had always been a person of faith, and believed that if we prayed to the deceased they would visit us and send us signs. God knows I was praying. Taking a slow deep breath, I knew in my heart she was safe. She was safe from pain and worries. The fight was over for her, Mom could rest now. No more hiding or pretending, she was free of it all. I was convinced she wanted me to know that she would always be with us. Witnessing this had given me peace. I knew that my mom was resting. Eventually, I drifted off from the exhaustion.

The next morning I had to tell my dad what happened. I expected he would get upset, but I also wanted him to know she was at peace. I explained to my dad what occurred, he suddenly began to cry. "I'm sorry Daddy, I didn't mean to make you cry," I said. "No, it's okay," he said. "I'm crying because your mother also came to me last night! It was the most beautiful vision I have ever seen. She was young again and so beautiful!" With no words to say, I wrapped my arms around him, as we both held each other and cried. "It's okay Daddy, she is always going to be with you. Just know she will always be by your side!" I hugged him as tight as I possibly could, I never wanted to let go. If I could have, I would have taken all of his pain away. My heart was overwhelmed with sorrow for him. It was validation enough to know my mother's beautiful soul had crossed over to a place where there would only be peace for her. This beautiful place we know as Heaven.

The following week was very trying for all of us, including the grandchildren. They were lost without their Mima. We were preparing to give her a beautiful send off. We made photo collages, rummaged through albums, and had the grandchildren, together, write the most beautiful eulogy. There were lots of tears and laughter as we all reminisced about this amazing person we had lost. It didn't seem real. We knew our lives were forever changed. As I went through her belongings I found photos that had been separated for each of my siblings, me and the grand-children. I couldn't believe it. She had them all sorted in Ziploc baggies, labeled with who they were for. She prepared to leave us, and made sure we had special memories to hold close to our hearts. She made sure all things were in order, that is what she did. I eventually came across that damn infamous envelope she was so insistent upon me mailing. I opened it to find that my Mom had canceled her previous life insurance policy to begin a new one, never mailing it in time, leaving us with no money for her burial. Now it all made sense. She was so adamant about me mailing it because she knew we would need the money. Unfortu-nately, the burial was a financial burden for my dad, but with the amazing friends and family we had in our lives we managed to pull it together. We gave my mother the most beautiful send off ceremony, which she deserved. The sadness was overwhelming, and her death shocking. There were times I didn't believe that I would not see my mother ever again and found myself thinking, *where do I go from here?*

Chapter 11

Mom's Fear, My Fight

Having to let go of my mom and accept her passing from such a horrific disease was painful and life changing. How can I describe what I felt? There are no words to express what I was feeling inside. I had never known this kind of grief. The grief that opens your heart to so much suffering, that you become numb. My family and I were still in a state of total shock. I had no way to rationalize what we went through, or how I was feeling. I was uncontrollable and filled with hostility. It was rage that burned inside of me. I harbored so much anger. I began to have anxiety attacks. I wanted to be able to rewind time so I could fix things. I would wake up in the middle of the night crying after having nightmares. That damn three letter word "why" kept flashing in front of me. I would look up to the sky and ask her, *why, why did you do this?* At a time in which I needed to be closer to God, I found myself not wanting to step foot inside of a church. I tried to support my dad and meet him at the Saturday 5 o'clock mass, but I was furious with God. All I could do was cry. So many people told me my feelings towards God were normal. Yet I asked myself, how could I blame God? This was my mother's choice, right?

Not only was I angry, but every time I looked at my dad, my heart shattered. My heart felt so much pain for him. I always knew him to be a pillar of strength, and now he was crumbling before me. He would lock himself inside the bathroom, for his bouts of tears. These were his moments of anguish that I did not want to hear, but did. He cried to her, "Why did you leave me, why? I'm all alone now." Endless days and nights echoed like this. I packed some belongings and decided to stay with my dad for a while. He was just too fragile to leave alone. I was worried about him so I spent many nights with my dad at the apartment. I would go into my mom's room and lay on the bed without her. This was something my mom and I would do all the time. I would grab her pillow and bury my face to muffle the sounds of my crying, hoping my dad did not hear me. I would have done anything to have her lying next to me again. Life was so lonely and empty without her. We all knew that this was the circle of life, that we can't live forever, but we can never be prepared for the loss of a parent especially the way I had lost mine.

As the days passed, I started to realize that my dad actually didn't need me around. He needed some personal space to cry when he needed to, and to get angry when he wanted to. He deserved distance from me and family to mourn his wife alone. He was certainly giving me subtle hints. He would say, "Why don't you and the boys go home? I'm fine." But I felt so guilty leaving him. His sorrow was killing me. He seemed depressed and lonely. I wanted to coddle him, do everything for him so that I could make his pain disappear. But the truth was not I nor anyone else would ever be able to take his pain away. He needed to grieve on his own time, at his own pace. This was normal, yet all so new to him. He was lost without my mom, she had done everything for him. My parents were a very "old school" couple and they had a beautiful marriage. One that I admired. They were high school sweethearts who created a beautiful life for themselves, always showing us nothing but love. My dad worked and mom stayed home to raise a family, she wanted to be the best wife and mother she could be. This is what she lived for and achieved. She really was an incredible wife and mother. My dad was so dependent on her in so many ways. I knew this was going to be difficult. I tried to go see my dad and cook for him as often as I could. I didn't want him eating alone, or spending nights looking at the empty chair that my mom would have sat on. It was situated next to him and was now abandoned. I began to teach my dad "new domestic tricks," so to speak. Slowly but surely, he began to do things he had never done before. He wanted to make my mom proud! I actually got the biggest kick out of him. I would get the phone calls . . . "Guess what, I just did a load of laundry," or "How do you boil the pasta?" I used to tease him, trying to make light of things. It was quite comical. He was so proud of himself. He even began to cook dinner, here and there, for me and the boys. He was determined to become independent, telling me, "I got it, I can clean the apartment on my own, go take care of yourself!" He would say, "You have your own things to do, I can't depend on you. I have to do it for myself now." I was so amused at the way my old-fashioned Italian dad became so house broken. Learning new tricks wasn't easy, especially at his age. This was my dad's way of portraying his strength to us. My father was always a hero in my eyes. Not only was he a cancer survivor, he had many other health issues along with surgeries that he took in stride. He never let anything knock him down. Have no doubt, this was one of the toughest things he ever had to face. With determination and faith, he was once again overcoming the many obstacles. I knew my mom was shining down on him brightly.

My father and I began to get closer than I could have imagined. We had deep conversations about life, love and happiness. He always gave me such profound advice and always worried about me as a single mom. He used to say to me, "Continue to surround yourself with only good people, and one day you will find love again." "You're a good person," he would tell me, "never give up on wanting more and always know your worth." I always wanted to believe those words, but he knew I was pessimistic when it came to finding love. He appreciated the fact that I had such a good group of friends that loved me and supported me. He was always giving me the best advice, but the very best piece of advice that he ever gave me was, "Go get yourself checked out, and beat this breast cancer before it gets you too! I don't ever want to see you go through it." My dad was truly concerned for me. His sister at the time was also battling breast cancer, so it surrounded us from both sides of the family. "Do what you have to do to save yourself," he said. I will never forget his words. "I will support you no matter what you decide to do, I don't want to see this happen to you one day." It was comforting to know that he turned his thinking around, and realized the importance of preventative care. He told me how he wished he had pushed my mom to be more proactive. Little did he know, precautionary measures were already the plan for me. The day I lost my mother was the day I knew my fight! Now that my dad had opened the door to the conversation and I saw how supportive he was going to be, I explained that I already had an appointment with Dr. Kadison. My dad was one hundred percent behind me from the day that I told him. I knew I could count on him and my brothers for support. My brothers also said to me, "do what you have to do to avoid this." They were just as concerned as I was. This was a reality for me now. Knowing the genetics of the women in the family, I also knew that my brothers were at high risk. For the first time in my life, I was seriously considering a prophylactic mastectomy. Some said this was too rash of a decision, but I didn't care what anyone thought. Until one had walked in my shoes, and felt the pain of losing a mother in four short days, no one had the right to judge me. I wasn't okay with living my life as if nothing was wrong, waiting for the storm to come. I needed to adjust my sails before the storm arrived, and be well prepared. To ignore the genetic facts that were staring me right in the face would be complete ignorance on my part. I begged my mom to be proactive, so why would I not practice what I preached?

I stood stern with my position and kept the appointment with the oncologist. I knew deep in my heart what had to be done in order to avoid the inevitable. Returning to Dr. Kadison, I told him my mom's news. Baffled by what she had done, he knew now more than ever, the importance of considering a prophylactic mastectomy. To no surprise, this was a preventative measure I knew I was facing. We had an in-depth conversation, weighing out all the options. Did I have choices? Of course. We could sit back and wait for the cancer to come, or we could take the bull by the horns. I already knew my decision . . . it was to beat the fuck out of cancer, before it got me. I was determined to escape this "beast," as I called it. He explained that even though I was BRCA negative, he was more concerned about the other genetic factors at play. He explained that the cancer hadn't skipped a generation, and this was a red flag. "You're like a ticking time bomb," he said to me. To be honest, I was panic-stricken. I trusted this man immensely. I trusted him with my life. I knew he would never steer me in the wrong direction. He was thorough. He spoke to me and looked out for me, as if I were family. This was the day I decided, I would fight. The fight for my right to have this surgery, to get it before the cancer got me. It was a fight that was fueled by the rage and anger in me from losing my mom. The fight that would be in honor of my mom. This was it, my decision was made and it was time to move forward. There was no one who could have changed my mind. I knew in my heart what needed to be done.

Dr. Kadison and I stayed diligent and on top of my routine check-ups. Like clockwork, I was constantly getting sonos and mammos as a preventative measure. We began to approach the insurance company about the surgery. They weren't complying, saying it was not necessary. Yet, it was clear as day that the family history was strong, and that it wasn't a matter of *if* I would be faced with breast cancer, but *when*. This battle wasn't short-lived, it carried on for a good amount of time. My doctor fought hard for me. He truly was an angel on my side. I was so blessed to have found such a compassionate doctor, one who understood my fears. He took me under his wing, and was always willing to go to bat for me. The insurance company fought us for about two years, and made it frustrating and difficult. After what seemed to be a really long and arduous battle, there was finally a breakthrough. Dr. Kadison called me with the news that the insurance company had finally approved the surgery . . . finally! *Could this really be happening?* This was exciting yet frightening at the same time. I took time to wrap my head around this, and I began to prepare myself mentally for the surgery. The date was set for November 17, 2015. I was terrified but it was time to start this journey. I called my dad to share the news. He was so happy for me, as he was always my biggest supporter. Unfortunately, not everyone in my family was as supportive. There were those who thought I should just ride it out and wait. Well, I wasn't willing to wait until it was too late. I alone lived with my fear. Watching my mother die so quickly had a tremendous impact on my state of mind. So much so, that I said "Nope, not me!" Surgery was the decision I chose for myself, and it was what was going to be. Did I doubt myself? Yes, of course. I would be lying if I said that I didn't. I talked myself into it, and talked myself out of it. My feelings were all over the place. I was petrified and had no idea what was to come or what I was in for, physically or emotionally. I guess you could say I was very fearful of the unknown. I was a single mom, so I didn't have the support of a spouse, nor did I want to burden my young boys with this. My dad was in his seventies, and in no condition to care for me. I was blessed to have family and friends that were supportive who offered to help. But I couldn't expect people to take me to appointments or take care of me. This was a choice I made and it was all on me. I knew I had to put my "big girl pants" on and fight. I was eventually very confident in what I was doing, the decision was made. I was plowing full steam ahead, no matter how frightened I was. Giving in to the fear was not an option. I was going to have to do some spiritual digging to find the strength for the road ahead.

With the surgical decision in place, I needed to find a top notch breast surgeon. Putting all my trust in Dr. Kadison, he referred me to an amazing plastic surgeon who specialized in the breasts. His name was Dr. Neil Tanna. The plan was to schedule my appointment rather quickly and meet with him. Before I knew it, the appointment day arrived, I was so nervous. I had a lump in my throat for the duration of the car ride to the office. As I walked through the medical office doors, the unknowns that I would face, forced me to find courage. Upon arrival the staff was nothing short of amazing. They were very welcoming, caring and recognized how nervous I was. Walking into the exam room, I was curious enough to look around at the posters and paraphernalia on the walls. I had no clue what it all meant. Then came the knock at the door and in walked Dr. Tanna, with this big smile and pleasant demeanor. He immediately calmed my nerves, making me feel comfortable. He was amazing. First he listened to my questions and concerns as he got to know me. He then explained the different options of breast reconstruction. He was sympathetic to my feelings and thoughts. As the patient, he constantly kept me in the forefront of the conversation. I never realized the many options there were for women. Apparently, Dr. Kadison and Dr. Tanna had already had conversations, and thought the best alternative would be to do a double mastectomy with tissue expanders to implants. Of course the decision was ultimately mine, but I knew I had to put my trust in these doctors. He explained that tissue expanders were the less traumatic way to reconstruct, allowing the body to heal as I moved along the process. This was all new to me, so I followed their lead and took their advice. I was going to go with their suggestions. I had not heard of these procedures, nor did I know anyone who had them done. Dr. Tanna and his team seemed to be very empathetic and thorough, leaving me feeling confident about the decision. He took his time to explain the details and asked if I had questions or concerns. Of course I did, and believe me I asked. My head was bursting with information. All this talk about scars, drains, the types of implants and sizes, and the surgeries was overwhelming. Sitting there alone, I tried to absorb and understand as much as I could without looking confused. I'll admit, I wished I had an extra set of ears in case I missed anything he said. It was one of the most difficult decisions I had to make alone. It was times like this that I'd wish I had someone to lean on. I felt alone yet knew I wasn't, I had incredible doctors committed to my mission. This made me feel so much more at ease.

After meeting him, I headed home and I was a basket case. For the first time, it all began to feel real. My stomach was doing flips. I was extremely nervous. I talked to my mom the entire ride home, praying for her and Grandma to guide me. Eventually, I called Dr. Tanna with more questions. He was always so patient with me. I thought, *how blessed am I to have these two amazing doctors by my side?* They were so caring and understanding of my fears. They kept reassuring me that I was in the best of hands. I absolutely loved their confidence. This made me feel safe and confident as well. Things seemed to be moving full speed ahead. The plan had been set. As the procedure day got closer, I kept reminding myself that this was the right thing to do. All pre-op testing was done, and the countdown had begun. Until the day I got the phone call . . . it was two weeks before the surgery. Dr. Kadison called to explain that the insurance company reneged the approval and they were not willing to cover the surgery. "On what grounds?" I wanted to know. He told me that they wanted more medical proof of my high risk. Imagine, they were claiming they needed more proof? What the hell did that even mean? More medical proof? I guess my grandmother, aunt, and mother weren't enough for them. Dr. Kadison then explained that they wanted me to go for genetic testing. That's what they considered medical proof? *Give me a fucking break,* I thought. "So let's do this," I said. "I'll do whatever it takes to get this done!" It was ridiculous, it seemed to be a game they were playing. I was furious. I was mentally prepared to do this, and then BAM! I walked onto a dead end street. They slammed on the breaks. Time to fight a little harder, I guess. Moving forward on this as quickly as we could, Dr. Kadison referred me to a genetic specialist. I began the tedious process of finding the DNA in the family that was causing breast cancer. If this was what they wanted, then it was what I would give them . . . "the proof." My doctor was already convinced this cancer was driven by a genetic factor, without any proof . . . let's give them what they want.

The appointment was made. I headed to the North Shore of Long Island to meet with the genetic specialist. Walking into the office I was full of anxiety. I wanted the proof that we needed to get this surgery approved. The genetic counselor was very kind, and assured me if there was a gene they would find it. As we thoroughly went through family history, it was very intriguing to see how they laid it all out. Wow, we had a lot of cancer in the family. Obviously, we knew it was coming from my maternal side of the family. The Chief of Hematology came down to meet me, and he said something that was striking. He told me that he didn't care what the blood work was going to show. He said he didn't need blood work to prove that this cancer was passing down directly to me. He said that if someone were to put a gun to his head and ask him if I would end up with breast cancer, without having the blood work results, he would say yes. That was so profound. It wasn't a matter of if I will ever get breast cancer, it was a matter of when. This confirmed that I was making the right decision. There was no doubt in my mind or concern that I was being rational. This was the second doctor who felt this way. With the family tree all laid out it was time to do the blood work. The real proof that was needed. They took about four vials of blood and it would take the lab around four weeks or so to deliver the results. The waiting game and anticipation began. I was so anxious to see what they would find, I wanted answers. I was so deep into this at this point, there was no turning back.

About four weeks went by, and I finally got the call I had been waiting for. It was the office, calling to make an appointment with me. Scheduling me as a priority, I was able to get in quickly. Arriving at my appointment, the Chief of Hematology came down to discuss the results. "So" he said. My stomach immediately dropped. "The good news is we found the DNA that we believe is linked to the breast cancer in this family. The bad news is that Lynch Syndrome is the mutation we have discovered. We also found that you have another unnamed cancer mutation." Astonished by what was just thrown at me, I asked, "What's Lynch Syndrome? And what do you mean, another mutation?" "Well, Lynch is the colon cancer gene, and it is connected to breast cancer and other cancers as well. As far as the other mutation, it's one that hasn't been named yet, and needs more research" he explained. My body was riddled with nervousness. "Hold on," I said. "I need to understand this. So, you're telling me I am not only at risk for breast cancer, but now I'm at risk for colon cancer, and possibly another type of cancer?" I tried so hard to fight back the tears, I really did. I could feel myself choking up. "Yes," he said. "But the good news is that some people never even know they have this gene, and find out when it's too late. You know it now, and will have to religiously get your colonoscopies. If you stay on top of it, and take preventative measures, you will be okay. It's important to find the polyps early, so it can be avoided." This didn't make me feel any better, quite honestly. *Was it supposed to?* This absolutely sucked! Yes, on the one hand they found the gene that had been causing havoc in my family. On the other hand, it was now my havoc! "We will never know if your grandmother or mother carried this gene. But if I had to bet, I would say yes," he said. "Because Lynch gets passed down from either your mother or father. Obviously it's very prominent on your mother's side. Your father's family doesn't show these types of cancers." Oddly enough, my maternal grandmother had many sisters, and a couple of them passed from cancers that Lynch was responsible for. We finally had an answer. I was so torn. A part of me felt relieved to have an answer, but another was distraught. This gene put me at risk for so many cancers.

To have to accept all this was overwhelming. I never expected these findings. Yes, genetically I expected to find a cancer gene, but this was more complicated than I could have imagined. With this information in hand, it was now time to approach the insurance company once again. *Let them try and deny me now*, I thought. The results were sent over to my doctor, who presented this to the insurance company. Now they would have the proof. How could they not approve this, right? Wrong . . . denied! Even with the cancer gene that was discovered, they still denied me. They wanted more medical proof. What more did they want? What other medical proof could we possibly provide? This was just idiotic. My doctor could not believe this nonsense. He told me that he personally called the insurance company to express his dismay. He did not understand how an insurance company would rather have a patient get cancer first and then cover the cost of treatment, when it was more beneficial for the patient and cheaper for the insurance company to be proactive. They did not care. No was no. It was absurd in my eyes. What more did they want from me? I had done everything they asked for, and followed the protocols. Little did they know, I wasn't giving up. Especially now knowing that I had this cancer mutation. It made my fight stronger and more important.

About another year had passed, and the fight was still on. It was a constant battle with the insurance company. Things were at a stand still. The only thing I could do for myself was to be diligent, always practicing my self exams. In the shower with the "soapy hands" technique was the best way to check for nodules. There was no such thing as being overly cautious. I was always on alert that any day cancer could sneak up on me. One day while practicing this method in the shower, I discovered a pea-sized nodule. This was a new finding. I was very familiar with my cystic breasts. I had never felt this one before. I immediately called Dr. Kadison and he had me undergo a sonogram and a mammogram as soon as possible. They did in fact discover a small nodule on the right breast. He was concerned. My breasts were very dense, and it was always difficult to see the nodules on a sono or mammo. The situation was getting very frustrating. My doctor had decided that he would do a biopsy to show some proof to the insurance company. He felt that if the biopsy showed something, the insurance company would have no choice but to approve the surgery (besides he needed to know what this was exactly). With this plan set we went ahead and did the first biopsy, which was unsuccessful. Painful as it was, the doctor didn't find what he needed. My doctor then referred me to another breast doctor. He believed that if anyone could get to it, she would be able to. She was one of the best. The nodule was in an awkward spot and hard to reach. So once again, greatly trusting his advice I went to see the secondary doctor. I was riddled with nerves and anxiety yet again. The first biopsy was no joke, and extremely painful. I knew what I was in for. Arriving for the appointment, I was checked in, and I waited patiently. I prayed, *please God let them reach this, and let it be nothing!* The nurse led me in, and settled me in the procedure room. "The doctor will be right in," she said. Once the doctor arrived, she proceeded to go through my history, asked all of the same questions that I had answered so many times before, and then began to take a look. Like before, it was very difficult to see, due to the fact that I had very dense breasts. She explained that it would be difficult to reach, but she would do her best. They marked the breast, and began to probe around. She probed and probed. I tried hard to stay still through the uncomfortable pain. It was almost impossible! Long story short, the best of the best couldn't reach this nodule. It was in such an awkward spot, she could barely see it, never mind reach it. With the pain beginning to feel intolerable, as she tried to maneuver and fish around, I began to sweat and go into a full blown panic attack. "Enough!" I shouted. "I can't take any more, please just stop." I had to shut it down. It was all so senseless. Sitting up trying to catch my breath, I began to break down. The doctor was very sympathetic to my situation, and understood my anger. Leaving there an emotional mess, I immediately called Dr. Kadison to tell him what had occurred. "So what's the next step?" I asked. He expressed that we would need to do an MRI. This would at least show that there was something there, and we would be able to present it to the insurance company. With this becoming all-consuming, I decided that a weekend away with the girls would be just the thing. With the MRI scheduled, I needed to escape and not think about anything. I headed down to New Jersey, *I would deal with this when I got back*, I thought.

The weekend came and went. I had a lot of laughs and relaxation, which was just what I needed. It was Sunday, and we decided to head back early. As I approached my apartment, I received a dreaded phone call. Something very tragic happened to my father. He was headed to the hospital. My and my family's faith was constantly being tested. I put myself on the back burner, to care for my dad. He needed me now more than ever. We spent days in and out of the hospital. His body was apparently shutting down from PTSD. I had never witnessed anything like this before. My dad became a priority, so I took time off from work to care for him. In the midst of this chaos, I was not focused on my situation at all. I was consumed with my dad and had not done the MRI. After weeks of hospitalizations and many complications, the doctors finally allowed my dad to go home. This was great news, but he was not out of the woods just yet. After contracting a staph infection, while in the hospital, he was sent home with an IV drip of antibiotics for several weeks. This was yet another hurdle in life for him to overcome. My father once again amazed me. He took things in stride, and did what he had to do. After a few more weeks he was settled and somewhat back to normal. He slowly began to recover. It was now time to get back to me.

It was around November, I was recovering from living in the midst of complete chaos. Suddenly, the unexpected, yet expected happened. In the middle of the night while I was at home sleeping, I suddenly had an itch under my armpit. It was so annoying that it woke me up. I stretched my arm out to scratch it, and to my surprise I felt a lump the size of a gumball. Immediately I panicked and jumped up! My entire body went numb. I sat there frozen in fear, I couldn't move. Coming out of a deep sleep, I thought . . . did I just feel what I thought I did? I reached back to feel it again, yup, there it was . . . a gumball-sized lump. I could literally feel my heart pounding out of my chest, like I had just run a marathon. I jumped out of bed and ran to the bathroom to take a look in the mirror. I remember I began to breathe heavily, I couldn't catch my breath. My immediate thought was, *"Oh my God it's here, it's here, it's here."* I was in complete panic mode. My mind began to race with every possible scenario. I was terrified. The worst of the situation was that it was the middle of the night, and I couldn't contact my doctor. I looked at the clock, realized it was only 3 a.m., and all I wanted to do was talk to my dad. I needed to speak to him, someone, anyone! I knew, in his frail state, if his phone rang it would frighten him. There was nothing I could do but sit and wait. Sitting in my chair in the dark, with my nerves rattled, I began to cry and beg, "please God don't let this be it!" I prayed to my mom, grandma, anyone who would hear me. I had to be quiet, I didn't want to wake my son. I spent the night getting up and down, going in and out of the bathroom to look in the mirror, pacing the floor, knowing that the doctor's office didn't open until 9 a.m. My nerves had me in motion. I kept thinking, *this is what I've been trying to avoid! It's fucking here, it's fucking here!* I had to stay calm, and I needed to pull myself together. I didn't want my son to see me upset. Waiting for what seemed to be an eternity, the sun began to finally rise. I got my son off to school, anxiously ran home and got dressed. I knew that once I called Dr. Kadison, he would want to see me immediately, and I wanted to be ready. Eventually 9 a.m. arrived. I called and as anticipated was given a morning appointment. I headed to work for a couple of hours first, I couldn't focus. I just wanted to get to the doctor. Finally, it was time to go. After I got checked into an examination room, Dr. Kadison walked in. He began to examine me and immediately asked why I hadn't done the MRI. I explained what happened with my dad, and he instantly sent me for an MRI stat. I was nervous and scared. I had not yet called my dad. I didn't want him to worry before I had any answers. While driving to the imaging center, I can honestly say I shook to my core. I was a nervous wreck. I didn't know what was going to happen, but I couldn't help but think the worst.

When I arrived, the tech immediately took me in. I headed to the back room to change and prayed to my mom. I needed her now more than ever. I felt completely alone. She had always been by my side for everything. All I could do was talk to her and hope that she heard me. This was my worst nightmare, and I felt helpless. Having to stay still for the MRI was a challenge. My body was shaking. The technician felt the lymph node, and saw the fear on my face. "Try to stay completely still," she said. "If you move I will have to redo it." I remember lying face down on the MRI table. As the machine began to move into the tube, the tears started streaming down my face. I thought about what all the women in my family had been through. Closing my eyes, I tried to take deep breaths to stay calm. It was difficult. The repetitive banging noise made me even more nervous. All along I thought to myself, *stay strong, just stay strong.* The MRI was completed and confirmed. They did indeed see a small mass in my right breast, which was the pea size nodule they had been trying to biopsy. In fact, there was a lymph node that was protruding under my right arm. My body was obviously reacting to something that was brewing. I was at the mercy of God. All I could do was pray it wasn't cancer. There were no words to console me. I was absolutely following my mom's genetic footprints. I was shaped from the same damn mold as my mother and grandmother. Now I was petrified, thinking about what I could potentially face.

Immediately, the results were sent over to Dr. Kadison. He called me to explain that it may be nothing or it could be something, but they wouldn't know until he was able to do the surgery. It was time to finally get this done. He was convinced, more than ever, that this was now an urgent matter and couldn't wait any longer. With the results in hand, the office personnel called the insurance company and told them the surgery was needed. They explained the results of the MRI, that there were no more games to be played, and no time to waste! Now we waited. Talk about anxiety. I continued to feel this lump under my arm. It was driving my anxiety to an entirely new level. I now had to tell my dad, my boys, and my family what was happening. I waited for my father to get home and I headed over. He had been in such a frail state and had finally bounced back. I now had to throw this at him. When I walked through the door he knew, by the look on my face, that something was wrong. I explained what happened to me over the last 24 hours, and I began to cry. Once again, being the pillar of strength that he always was, he wrapped his arms around me and held me tight. "Stay strong for me," he said, "Come on, it's going to be okay, you have to stay positive! You're a strong person, don't let this break you!" He knew more than anyone else, the fear that I had. This was my worst nightmare, and he knew exactly what I was thinking. I didn't have to say it, he just knew. I felt so bad that after all he had been through, he now had to deal with this. How much more could this family live through? Why was it that our faith was constantly being tested? Nothing ever seemed to go right lately. All I wanted was for the damn surgery to be approved, especially now that something was lurking inside of me.

It was the day before Thanksgiving, I was busy at work when my phone rang. I saw Dr. Kadison's name and immediately my heart dropped. I knew I had to answer it. This was the phone call I had been waiting for. I ran to the back room and I answered, "Hello?" "Hi Joanne, it's Dr. Kadison. Where are you right now?" he asked. "I'm at work," I replied. "I need to talk to you. I need you to sit down," he said. "Okay, I'm sitting." *What the hell is going on?* "Are you ready for this?" he said. I began to shake. "I have some good news I wanted to tell you myself . . . your surgery was finally approved!" I couldn't speak. My first reaction was tears of relief! *Was this for real?* I couldn't believe the words I was hearing. "Dr. Kadison, for real? They finally approved it, we actually won this battle?" I asked. "We did it, it's finally going to be done," he said. He explained that, at this point, they really didn't have a choice but to approve it. The evidence that something was materializing was profound. Needless to say, I couldn't thank him enough for fighting for me. He wasn't just an advocate for me, he was an angel on my side. I was beyond lucky, from day one, to have him advocating for me. I never met a more humane doctor, one that was willing to do whatever it took for his patients. So attentive and considerate that he even picked up the phone to call me himself. I was truly blessed. Now the ball was finally rolling. Dr. Kadison said he would have the secretary get back to me with available dates. I also needed to come into the office to discuss what exactly would be done. I needed to see the breast surgeon again, as well. I went from sitting idle to plowing forward. I immediately called my dad, to share the "good news," so to speak. My dad was always supportive and never second guessed my decision. He never wanted to see me go through what all the women in the family had gone through. He constantly reminded me of the strength he knew I had. His words meant everything to me. "Daddy, do you think Mom is proud of me, not letting fear stand in the way?" I asked. He began to cry. "She will be with you every step of the way, and so will I," he said. He reminded me that when things got rough, to talk to her, that she would be there listening. My dad was my world. He always knew the right things to say to me. Then of course, with his silly personality, he had to lighten the mood. "Hey, don't make those things too big now, you don't want to look like Dolly Parton," he said. I went from crying to cracking up! I just loved him so. I knew it was going to be okay, as long as he was by my side. Yes ma'am, it was time to kick some ass! I was scared because I didn't know what they would find, or what was in store for me. I knew, for sure, it was going to be difficult in many ways.

I was a single mom of two, working seven days a week most of the time to try and make ends meet. *How was I financially going to afford to take time off?* I had many surgeries ahead of me . . . *how the hell was I going to do this?* I realized that when you don't have a choice, you find a way. I began to work a little harder to save some extra money, so I could take the time off I needed to recover with a clear mind. I was willing to do anything to make this happen. Little did I know just how many surgeries were ahead. Maybe, I was better off not knowing. I may have had second thoughts. But this was it, it was time to summon all my courage and strength and do this. This was the point of no return! That same day, Dr. Kadison's secretary called me back with a date. The surgery was set for December 14th. Something that was such a long battle, now seemed to be happening so fast! Things were getting real. I knew that there was a sense of urgency, but I didn't expect it to be so soon. I went into full panic mode. Christmas was just around the corner. I needed to get things done quickly. The next couple of weeks flew by between running back and forth to doctors, working, shopping and preparing. I didn't have time to mentally think about anything, maybe that was a good thing. I had to get all my ducks in a row. There was no time to sit and contemplate, or worry. There was so much to do, and a million things to think about. I was completely naive. I knew that I needed to be fully prepared. I had a full list of questions I put together.

What's the recoup time?

How will I sleep, will I need a special pillow or chair?

How will I shower, can I do it alone?

Can I blow dry my hair?

How will I empty the drains?

What will my scars look like?

Will I be able to cook, or even lift my arms?

Do I need special clothes?

What's the recovery like?

When will I be able to drive?

How will I get to my follow up appointments?

The list was endless! I began to prepare meals for my son, who lived with me, my dad and me. I bought myself a couple of button down shirts, because I was told I wouldn't be able to lift my arms. I made sure I had comfy pajamas to lounge in for a couple of weeks. I put some things together to keep myself occupied while I was homebound. I was preparing for the tsunami of events that was coming my way. I filled the pain med scripts, so they were there for me when I came home (subconsciously knowing I would never use them). I lined up rides for my son to get to and from school. There was so much to do in what seemed to be such a short period of time. Who had time to even think about the surgery? I just kept counting down the days, reminding myself every morning, *you got this girl*. I went through moments of calm and also moments of dread. There were tears of joy, and tears of fear. I was a mixed bag of emotions. I had many, many conversations with my mom and grandmother asking them to guide and protect me. And of course God, the ultimate protector. My mom always had such a presence. I always felt her around me, along with my grandmother. Since the loss of my boyfriend, I became a true believer in signs from above. I always believed our loved ones only left us in the physical form, but remained in the spiritual state with us. Every day seemed to bring a new "sign". I truly believed I was making the right decision.

Chapter 12

Beginning My Journey

December 14th, 2016 had finally arrived. I don't think I got a wink of sleep. I was lying in bed, trying to keep myself in a calm state of mind, not allowing myself to fall into a deep sleep. I even tried to do some meditation techniques that a friend taught me. I was waiting for time to pass, while constantly looking at my phone wishing the night away. I had to be at the hospital extremely early in the morning. The surgery was set for the earliest time slot. Finally, after what felt like an eternity, my alarm went off. I jumped up and sat at the edge of the bed talking to myself and praying. *Okay, you got this girl, it's going to be okay.* This was the day I knew I had to put *my faith over fear.* I prayed to God and anyone who was listening to me, "please keep me safe." This was the first day of my new lease on life. I had to dig real deep, deep down inside and pull every ounce of strength I had to be able to get through what was to come. I kept telling myself, *Jo, when your back is up against the wall, this is what you do. Fight girl, fight.* I was pep-talking myself. One thing I did know, this was going to be a journey like no other, unlike no other path I had ever walked. The first thing I had to do to prepare was to take a shower. I had to shower, (as I did the night before) with special antibacterial soap. I needed to scrub and sterilize my body. I also washed and blew my hair dry, knowing it would be days before I would be able to do it on my own again. Putting on my new cozy Christmas pajamas that I had just bought, I was ready to go. I waited for my ride to arrive, it was a really cold morning and there was snow on the ground. I continued to pray and tried to keep myself calm. It was early in the morning when I hopped into the car, so there was no traffic. We made it to the hospital pretty quickly. Oddly, I was so calm I couldn't explain it. I was in a good frame of mind. You would think I would be a complete basket case, but I wasn't. I felt calm and confident. Confident in my decision, and confident that it was all going to be okay.

I previously mentioned that I was a believer in mediums and connecting with our loved ones who have passed. Well, one day before my surgery I went to drop off a Christmas gift to a beautiful woman, Lynn, whom I called a friend. She happened to be a medium. My mom, of course being a strong presence, came through. She gave me nothing but beautiful messages. She told me it would all be okay, that I was in the best of hands, and all my angels would be surrounding my bedside the day of the surgery. She told me to never worry only trust, and that I did. I trusted this team of doctors immensely. Not for one second did I doubt I was in great hands. I also knew I was having this surgery at a top notch hospital.

As I walked into the lobby, I noticed the hospital was so

quiet you could hear a pin drop. We were greeted by the security guard who directed us to the check-in area. As soon as I arrived the nurses immediately took me in and began to prep me for surgery. All the paperwork had been taken care of, which made the process a little easier. Once I stepped behind the curtain the ball was rolling. I swear, there was no time to even think about the "what if's". These nurses had the routine down pat. I think they must have asked me my name and birthdate over thirty times. I laughed every time they did. I was hooked up to the I.V. fluids, and I met the anesthesiologist. What a great man, I will never forget him! He was a big, tall, strong guy with an amazing smile and a wonderful personality. I believe he was of Hispanic descent, I can still hear his accent. Every time he spoke to me, he called me "Mama." I don't remember his name, but for certain I remember his face. He was there to make sure I knew he was going to take good care of me. His confidence was my calm. He began to ask me a bunch of questions, then reassured me that everything was going to be okay. This was a time consuming surgical procedure and I am asthmatic, he knew that this worried me. He made me laugh, yet was very serious and professional. I knew that he was trying to keep me calm. "Remember I have two beautiful boys I need to wake up for," I told him. He looked at me and said, "I got you Mama, I promise. You're going to have a good nap," he chuckled. He smiled and said, "I'll be back for you in a little bit," As he walked out, in came Dr. Kadison, the angel by my side. He stood there with his hands folded and smiled at me. "Are you ready?" he asked. "As ready as I'll ever be," I said, laughing. He sat down and proceeded to cover everything precisely, step by step . . . how long the surgery would be, exactly what they would be removing, the possibility of saving the nipples, or the possibility of removing them, where the incisions would be, what to expect when I came to, it went on and on. It was a laundry list of information. As I sat there and listened, I could slowly feel a lump forming in my throat. Trying my best not to cry, I could feel it getting worse by the minute. Dr. Kadison looked at my son, who was sitting there and said to him, "I want you to know that your mom is making the right decision here today. If this were my wife or daughter sitting here, I would do the same for them. This isn't a choice anymore, it's what needs to be done." He also began to explain that what he found would determine the next steps. Besides removal of the breast tissue, if any lymph nodes looked suspicious they would be removed as well. Depending on what he saw when he removed the breast tissue, he would do his best to try and save the nipples as long as the margins looked clean enough. Honestly, I didn't care at this point. *Just do what needs to be done*, I thought. He also explained that once he was done removing all the breast tissue that was when the breast surgeon, Dr. Tanna, would come in and put the expanders in place. The conversation was over, and now . . . it was time. Dr. Kadison looked at me with his reassuring smile. "Okay, any questions?" I didn't have any. These were things we had previously discussed, I was ready to go. I put my trust in these incredible doctors. I had no doubts. He asked everyone to leave the room for a minute. He opened my gown and began to 'mark me' like an etch-a-sketch board. Once it was done he looked at me and said, "Okay, I'll see you in the O.R." Dr. Kadison walked out and the nurse came in. "Okay," she said. "Give your son a kiss, tell him you love him, we're going to take you in now." This was the time to hold back the tears. I couldn't let my son see me in a weakened state. No way, not now! Swallowing the lump in my throat, I put on a calm face and kissed and hugged him. I wanted to be a pillar of strength now, and not show my vulnerability. Although people say it's okay to show your weakness, this wasn't the time. It was always important to me, especially as a single mom, to show strength to my boys. My son left the room and so did the nurse, she would be right back. I sat there for a minute all alone, and reality finally hit. Tears began to roll down my cheeks. There was no need to hold back. I wished my mom was with me at that moment. I began once again, to talk to her and my grandma. Being the faithful person that I was, I knew they heard me. I kept trying to remind myself that I wasn't alone. I strongly believed my angels were with me. I could envision all my loved ones surrounding me while in surgery. The anesthesiologist finally came back to get me. He was full of positivity, which was just what I needed. He saw me sitting there with tears in my eyes. "Let's go Mama," he said. Bending down he said to me, "Hop on, Mama." He was offering me a piggyback ride! I began to laugh. Of course I did, gown and all! "You got this," he said as he carried me off to the O.R. This man, in that very moment, was my knight in shining armor! Okay, I wasn't riding off into the sunset on a white horse, I was riding off to the O.R., but to me he was the light I needed. He was such a reinforcement, he relaxed my nerves. Along with many others, my life was in his hands. Entering the O.R. I was surprised to find the room a little small, yet packed with a team of nurses. Maybe that's why it seemed so small to me. Even though they had masks on, I saw their eyes squinting as they smiled at me. "Good morning," they each said. I got up on the table and of course it was freezing. They put the warming blanket on me right away, which was welcoming. It was routine when having surgery. I felt one of the nurses rubbing my legs. They were shaking terribly. I couldn't keep them flat on the table. Yes, I was scared crap! My mind raced a mile a minute. My heart pounded through my chest, I closed my eyes so I wouldn't see all the instruments and the bright lights. I tried to keep calm, and told myself to breathe deeply. The anesthesiologist was now standing behind me. He hovered over, placed his arms around my head and very quietly said "Okay Mama, let's say a prayer." And so we did. I prayed to anyone who would hear me. I kept thinking, *could these doctors and nurses be any more compassionate?* They were just incredible. What an amazing team of professionals they were. This was a specialized center for women and these types of surgeries; maybe that's why they were so caring. They faced this on a daily basis. It couldn't be easy for them. I have had many surgeries, but never this type of experience. God only knows how many patients they help go through this, and far worse at that. It must have been as difficult for them, as it was for me. Closing my eyes while they prepared me, I envisioned my mom, grandma and all the beautiful angels surrounding and protecting me. I began to feel a warm flush flow through my body, feeling a little loopy and sleepy. The doctors entered the room, reassuring me this was all going to be okay. Without fighting, I closed my eyes, I took a deep breath, prayed to my mom, and vaguely heard people talking. I drifted away leaving it all up to God.

It is crazy that no matter how many hours you're under anesthesia, it feels like minutes. The surgery lasted about six hours. While in the recovery room, I opened my eyes to peek and thought, *am I done?* I came to realize it was over. I remember it felt like I had just gotten run over by a bulldozer. That's the only way to describe the impact of this surgery. I had not heard anyone call my name, or maybe I just don't remember. I opened my eyes again and the nurse saw me. "Oh, you're awake," she said. "Surgery is over, you are in the recovery room. Just relax and don't try to move." I was heavily sedated, I wasn't going anywhere. All I wanted to do was sleep. Suddenly I began to feel extremely nauseous. Too weak to call the nurse, I began to heave. The nurse immediately came over and gave me something for the nausea. The pain was so intense, I didn't have the energy to heave again! The medicine seemed to work, and I was able to rest. Drifting in and out, I remember seeing my son leaning over the railing asking me to wake up. I opened my eyes to see him standing there, "Mom, it's all over!" Honestly, I didn't care, I just wanted to sleep. The anesthesiologist had been right, this was definitely a good nap. Who wanted to wake up at this point? Just let me sleep! Every once in a while I would be woken up by the nausea, and this sudden urge to urinate. The nausea was the worst part; I don't do well with pain meds, or anesthesia. I tried to keep my eyes closed and sleep. Hours drifted by, and it was finally time to move to my hospital room. I pretty much slept through the entire process. I vaguely remember being in the elevator, before I knew it I opened my eyes and I was in my room. I slowly came out of the anesthesia, looked to my left and there was my dad sitting quietly in the chair. He was so happy to see me. He just leaned over with red bloodshot eyes and kissed me. "How do you feel sweetheart?" he asked. "I don't know, right now I'm good. When the drugs wear off, I'll let you know," I said jokingly. He chuckled. He was so relieved to see me out of surgery. I looked out the window and noticed it was dark. It was as if time did not exist. I really didn't want my dad to stay long. I worried about him driving home so late by himself. By this time the nurses were coming in and out to get me hooked up and settled. "I'm hungry and dying of thirst," I said. "Okay let's sit you up a little so you can eat," I heard. My family had brought me some soup and crackers, which was just what I needed. The pain of adjusting the bed alone was numbing. I couldn't lift my arms to even grab the spoon. Everyone was so helpful, and I was able to get some food down. You would have thought I ran a marathon . . . I was exhausted just from eating. After I ate, all I wanted to do was sleep. I swear I thought I was in a five-star hotel. The hospital was so beautiful. It had a big screen T.V., a couch and a recliner for my family. I told everyone to head out, I wanted to get some rest. With that the nurses came in to check my vitals and they gave me some more pain meds, which knocked me out. It was so quiet and peaceful. I didn't realize there was another world right outside my door. The night went by, and the nurses were very quiet as they came in and out. For the most part I slept well.

The next morning the plan was to get me up and walking so that I could head home the following day. I thought they were out of their minds! How the hell could they send me home like this? Insurance protocols say so. As I was beginning to wake in the morning, I began feeling this odd pain in my shoulder. The same pain that I felt when I had the bleeding before my hysterectomy. I couldn't help but wonder if something was wrong. This type of pain was always a red flag for me. I called for the nurse and I explained what I was feeling. She then said, "Okay let's try to sit you up a little." Again, I told her what I was feeling, and that I thought something may be wrong. She replied that this was all normal. I had a very big surgery. As she began to sit me up, I told her that the pain meds were making me dizzy and nauseous. I asked her to shut them down, so that I would be able to walk. With all my prior surgeries I never took pain medications, I would only take Tylenol. I don't do well with pain meds. The nurse insisted that I needed them and that I would be okay. Against my better judgment I tried to stand up, and that's when

I lost it. I began to vomit and sweat. She immediately had to lay me back down. My head was in a complete spin! I just knew it! "I told you," I said to the nurse. She explained that I needed to be able to get up, walk the hallway, and allow her to help me with what is called a "half shower." She believed I would be able to do this without the pain meds. It took some convincing on my part, but after a bit of pleading and coaxing she finally shut down the pain med IV. She insisted that this was major surgery, and I needed pain medicine. But I knew my tolerance level, and knew I couldn't function with these drugs in me. I told her that I would never be able to walk as long as the meds were in my system. Slowly, I began to feel better as the nausea and dizziness faded, but the pain in my shoulder was concerning. I told the nurse again that it was getting worse. The pain was now in my right breast. Thinking something may be wrong, she called the doctor. By this time I was able to get up with assistance. I walked a little and showered with the help of the nurses. With the pain increasing, she decided to take a peek under the bandages. I can still remember the awkward feeling. As she unzipped the 'corset' bandage, it felt like I was empty. That's the only way to describe it. I refused to peek. I did not want to look. She began to gently feel around. "Does this hurt right here?" she asked. "Yes," I said. In fact, it hurt really bad. It felt like needles in my right breast, what was left of my breast. She said there seemed to be a little bit of a hematoma. She needed to put another call to the doctor to tell him what she had seen. I knew it! I know my body, and I was familiar with this pain. I really didn't think too much of it, I just thought it was a little bit of bleeding.

Before I knew it, Dr. Tanna walked in along with a few interns. He asked if having the interns in the room was okay, so they could also take a look. He began to unzip the bandage. Feeling around and touching the area, he said that I did, in fact, have a small bleed, and he would reach out to Dr. Kadison to discuss what needed to be done. He believed that more than likely, they would have to go in and drain it. *Are you fucking kidding me*, I thought. "Does this mean I have to be put under anesthesia again?" I asked. "Yes, but it will be quick, it shouldn't take too long," he said. "We have no choice but to go in and drain the blood." Well that was it, I broke down. I completely lost it. And the more I cried the worse the pain got. My family was not with me yet. I was alone and scared. I grabbed my cell phone, while crying uncontrollably, and called my dad. He answered immediately. I couldn't speak. He heard me crying. "What's the matter, sweetheart?" he asked. I had to pull myself together. I couldn't get the words out. I managed to calm myself down and explained the situation to my dad. "Please, I need you to come right now, I'm so scared," I cried. "You have to get here before they take me in." As I was hanging up with my dad, Dr. Kadison came in to take a look. It was definitely a bleed, and like Dr. Tanna said it had to be drained. This was a risk of any breast surgery, it had to be done. "How can I possibly go home tomorrow?" I asked. Obviously . . . I couldn't. He explained that I would be in the hospital until I was okay to leave, and I shouldn't be worried about being discharged. He made me feel better, because that was my biggest concern. I was afraid that when I got home, I wouldn't be able to help myself. So it was decided, I needed to go back to the O.R. The nurses came in to tell me what time they would be taking me down. This was shaking me, I was really afraid at this point. Unable to pick up the phone and lean on my mom was upsetting me. At this time in my life, I needed her. I was crying so much, I could feel my body tightening. I needed to call someone who I knew would relax me. I called Fran. Calling

Fran was the right decision. She was very level headed and rational. She talked me off the ledge. She explained that these types of bleeds are common and assured me it would be okay. My fears were still real, but I knew I had to stay calm. Crying was making the pain worse. It was an extremely difficult time, I was an emotional mess. My dad arrived just in time to see me before they took me to the surgical unit. He was trying to keep me relaxed, but the pain was getting unbearable. My emotional state was making it worse. Seriously, how much more can one face? I felt better knowing that my dad was with me. I began to calm down on the way to the O.R. I convinced myself that this was cake compared to what I had just gone through. As we entered through the doors, there was another anesthesiologist, a very nice man who took the time to explain to me that I wouldn't be under long. He told me I would feel groggy when I woke up and tried to make conversation. He was definitely trying to distract me. Before I knew it, I had drifted off taking that deep breath that put me into slumber.

"Joanne, wake up, you're all done." As I came to, I immediately noticed that the pain in my shoulder and chest was gone. The nurse checked on me frequently, asking me how I was feeling. Shockingly, I was surprised to find that I was feeling pretty good. While in the recovery room my family was able to come in and I was happy to hear my son's voice over the phone. I was relieved that I was feeling much better. I knew I had been through the worst of it, it could only be up from here on in. I stayed in the recovery room for a little bit, then I was brought back up to my room. My dad and my son were there waiting for me. My dad was sprawled out on the recliner; the poor thing was mentally exhausted. He was so happy to see me and I was so happy to see him! By this point I was starving, I needed to eat something to build some strength. This time I did not allow the nurses to hook me up to pain meds (my doctors thought I was crazy, by the way). I wanted to be able to get up and walk the hallways, and I couldn't do that on the drugs. After getting some food down, I was able to stand, walk quite a few times, even though my legs felt weak. I knew how important it was to move. Every time I took a stroll, my dad would walk with me and hold my hand, the nurse had me by the arm, and I held onto the IV pole for balance. This was my dad's way of saying,"I got you!" He wasn't a mushy guy, he was a man of very few words at times. These little gestures let me know he was there for me, and in his own way he always let me know how much he loved me.

I started to feel more alert and stable. Slowly I got stronger, which was keeping me in good spirits. I kept reminding myself that the worst of this was over, and everyday would be a new day of healing. My phone began to ring with friends and family checking in on me. This made the day go by quickly. Day turned into night, and it was time to get some rest. Sending everyone home, the nurses got me up a few more times, and I was able to sit in the recliner for a while. I was feeling pretty good. My spirits were up, and I was hopeful to be going home the next day.

In the morning, the doctors were in to make their rounds. They needed to open the bandage to check for any bleeding. Thank God everything was looking good. The doctor explained to me again that what happened was always a risk with any surgery. At that point, I was just happy that I made it through. I was so grateful to have these incredible doctors taking care of me. Dr. Kadison gave me the good news . . . I was approved to go home. Before leaving, we went over what I should expect. As the day went by I felt stronger and stronger. The social worker paid me a visit that morning, bringing me a cute little gift bag along

154

with some emotional support. She shared some beautiful words of encouragement with me. I was so happy to be going home, yet nervous at that same time. I knew going home meant I would be alone, and expected to stand on my own two feet. Excited, I called my dad and told him what time to come. The nurses were in and out of the room, trying to get all the paperwork in order. They also gave me what felt like a hundred instructional rules to follow. They showed me how to empty out drains. This was, by far, going to be the worst part of the at-home care. The dreadful drains! *How was I going to do this?* I tried to mentally wrap my head around everything I needed to do. How to change my dressings was also another thing that threw me for a loop. I did not want to see myself . . . at all. I was even told by a good friend, do not look in the mirror! You have to give yourself time. I knew this was something I had to mentally prepare myself for. It would be difficult to see my body. It was the body image that troubled me, not the incisions, blood, stitches, none of that mattered to me. Already anticipating that this was going to be difficult, I definitely wasn't ready. I didn't care what anyone said, you can never be prepared to see your body dismantled. Unless you've been through this, you could never fully understand it. Filled with determination to plow through, with strength not tears, I reminded myself that I was stronger then I knew.

Anxiously waiting for my ride, I ate some breakfast. I couldn't wait to get going. My dad arrived at the hospital, on a really cold day with snow in the forecast. In fact, it had already begun to snow. I was extremely nervous about the ride home. As we were preparing to leave, the roads began to get even more slick. All packed up and ready to go, the nurse helped me into the wheelchair to bring me to the car. Wheeling me down, she suggested I sit in the back seat of the car, due to the fact that I was unable to wear a seat belt. She propped me up with pillows, making sure I was comfortable, and off we went. I begged my dad to stay in the right lane and to take it real slow. I was so damn nervous, and we had a bit of a ride. I kept envisioning someone rear-ending us, thinking that would be a really bad situation. We arrived home safely. My dad and son Christian, who lived with me, got me down the stairs, into the apartment, unpacked and situated. They sat me up on the recliner with pillows all around me. I seemed to be doing okay. The pain was tolerable at this time, controlled only with Tylenol. With nothing to be done, except for me to rest, I told my dad to go home. I had my 16-year-old son with me. I knew if I needed anything he would help me. My dad was so worried, but he only lived blocks away. If I needed anything he could zip over quickly. Besides, I had prepared meals that were in the freezer. *Dear God,* I thought as I sat there, *How the hell am I going to do this?* This was going to be a long process and reality was now sinking in. I had purchased a bunch of adult coloring books for myself, and I planned to watch every Hallmark Christmas movie there was. I tried to prepare for this as much as possible, but you can never be a hundred percent prepared. Throughout the day, family and friends were calling to check on me. I had really great people in my life that went above and beyond. It was so nice to see how I was truly loved and how much people cared. The first few days were definitely the biggest challenge and pretty difficult for me. Not only mentally, but physically as well. I wasn't the type to sit still. I was already getting antsy thinking about how many days I had of sitting idle. The process of emptying the drains was proving to be a challenging one. I had no choice but to ask my son for help, until I could get familiar with the process. After seeing how difficult it was for him, I knew I had to accomplish it on my own. I wasn't fair to rely on him. This was all on me. Changing the bandages was the most difficult part of the care as I had anticipated it would be. I wasn't prepared to see myself this way. Every time I would open the surgical bra, the anxiety would kick into high gear. I would avoid the mirror at all costs, doing my best to change the bandages as quickly as possible so I wouldn't see the "new" me. Showering seemed to be the easiest chore of all. Before I had the surgery, I changed the shower head to a hand-held making life so much easier. I was managing these difficult hurdles, and I was proud of myself!

It was now December 19, and time to go visit Dr. Tanna for the first post-op checkup. Since I was not able to drive yet, my good friend Vicki offered to take me. As we walked in the door, I was feeling pretty good. I was quickly taken to the back and pre-pared to see the doctor. Within a few minutes Dr. Tanna walked in (always with a smile), asking me questions about how I was feeling. "Okay, let's take a quick look," he said. This is where my heart began to flutter. I wasn't prepared to really see myself. He began to open the surgical bra and remove the bandages. When the surgical bra was removed, I had this empty, numb, hollow feeling. It felt like everything was falling, as if gravity was taking over. He seemed to be happy with the healing and the way everything looked. I absolutely avoided looking down, at all costs. Instead, I watched my girlfriend's face for her first reaction. "You look great," Dr. Tanna said. "Yeah, you think so?" I asked nervously. Then I looked at my girlfriend. "Tell me honestly, how do I look?" "Jo, you really look good, I wouldn't lie to you," she said. Not that I didn't believe Dr. Tanna; it was just a girl thing I guess. Girlfriends are always brutally honest, right? She made me feel so much better, even though I am sure she was sugar coating it a smudge. Seriously, how could I look good? I just had my breasts removed. There was no "looking good." After examining the incisions, Dr. Tanna decided that he would remove a couple of the drains in another week or so. These drains played an important role in healing. They were annoying as all hell, but they needed to stay in longer. Dr. Tanna and I began to discuss the filling of the tissue expanders. This was the next phase. I remember thinking, *what the hell am I in for?* I would rather have left it to the element of surprise. Sometimes in this type of situation the unknown is better. I also reminded myself, I had to welcome what was to come. The fillers were part of the process we had discussed. I was anxious to get things moving. The visit went really well. We set up the next appointment date for the following week and headed out. This simple visit exhausted me. I couldn't believe how tired it made me feel. All I wanted to do was go home to my recliner.

Returning home, I had some time to reflect and consider what lay ahead. I reminded myself of the strength I needed to find. I would give myself pep talks and also think to myself, *why don't I stay flat? I mean, why not? My grandmother did. No one ever really knew she was flat, other than the immediate family. Wouldn't be so bad, right?* It never defined who she was, and I would never let it define me. I would rationalize with my thoughts thinking, *there are more women than I probably realize who have chosen to stay flat.* But deep down inside, I knew I was too much of a vain person to go that route. This was a moment when I allowed my fears to stand in the way of what I needed to do. I never spoke to anyone about my feelings, because who would actually understand me? The only person who would was my grandmother. Unfortunately, getting her advice was not possible. I never even discussed the option of staying flat with either of my doctors. These were the times I wished I belonged to some sort of support group or had a mentor. Having a sympathetic ear would have been helpful. I was not going to second-guess my decision. I was definitely moving forward with the filling of the tissue expanders.

December 22, it was time for another appointment. Again I depended on my gracious girlfriend Vicki for a ride. We headed back to Dr. Tanna to remove some drains. This was exciting because I hated them. I knew how important they were, but they were absolutely annoying and disgusting. They felt so funky hanging out of my body. It was truly amazing what the body could endure. I shared with my girlfriend that during my recent visit with Dr. Kadison, he reviewed the results of the pathology report with me. I explained that the doctor had removed a few suspicious lymph nodes on both sides, and that there were findings of atypical cells. We both agreed, and she reaffirmed me, that the decision I made was indeed the right one. Her words erased any doubt I may have had. These cells were lurking and it would have been a matter of time before the cancer would have surfaced.

Arriving at the appointment, everything was moving along smoothly. I had some swelling on the left breast but this was normal due to the trauma, otherwise things were healing nicely. It was time to remove a couple of the drains. Unfortunately, not all of them as I had hoped for, but at least there would be only two left. *Baby steps Jo, baby steps!* I always had to remind myself this process was slow. My next appointment was set for a week later, and off we went. I made up my mind that I would return to work slowly, not telling my doctor my intentions. I did not think he would have approved. As a single mom it was what I needed to do. I was confident that I knew my body, and I would not push myself. I purchased a few button down shirts, and some bulky tops to camouflage my breasts. I was all wrapped up, you couldn't tell I had surgery. I was super conscious of my look, and it made me very uncomfortable. I wore leggings and tucked the remaining drains into the leggings. They held the drains in place. Work definitely proved to be difficult, but if I felt tired I simply went home. I was so sleep deprived that it made working more difficult. Sleeping on a recliner was uncomfortable, and my sleeping pattern was affected by the surgery. I watched TV all night, due to my insomnia. It was horrible. I thought work would put me back into some sort of a routine, and give me a sense of normalcy. I reminded myself on a daily basis what my beautiful friend Lynn, who was the medium, had said . . . "every day you put your feet on the ground, remind yourself how beautiful and loved you are, and that you can do this!" And that is exactly what I did, everyday. I looked for the flame to light the fire in me everyday, and became more fierce and much stronger with every step I took.

Chapter 13

Walk With Me

It was the end of December and time for the next appointment with Dr. Tanna to remove the last two drains. I was beyond thrilled. The skin began to heal around the drains, which made it more difficult to remove them. This was by far no picnic. I was sweating and wiggling around as Dr. Tanna worked his magic, it had to be done. One of my drains seemed to be a little bit tangled. With a little pulling and tugging the drain was finally out. To my surprise, Dr. Tanna decided it was time to begin the process of filling the tissue expanders, in about a week or so. I didn't ask many questions, I was better off not knowing. I simply made the appointment and headed out. No sense in causing myself unnecessary anxiety, especially over something that was totally out of my control. I began to have some uneasiness and panic attacks, which I figured was normal. How could I not? I dealt with it as best as I could and carried on. Removing the last of the drains was mentally rewarding. I was happy and felt like it was a big step in the healing process. Most significantly and affecting, it was a door that forever closed on the multiple stages of this surgery. I could put that part of my life behind me. I was surprised and pleased at how smoothly everything seemed to be going. I had heard plenty of horror stories about what some women had to endure, and considered myself extremely lucky to have encountered just minor hiccups. The holidays passed and the new year had begun. I did a lot of healing and resting. My body needed it.

January 12, 2017, was a big day for me. It was time to begin the process of filling the tissue expanders. This procedure would slowly expand my breast skin, allowing room for the implants. I had decided to drive myself to the appointment. I couldn't keep depending upon people, this was something I knew I would eventually have to do. So I got in my car and took it slow. I arrived with no problems at all, I was relieved. What I didn't realize was that when filling the expanders there was a possibility of it being painful. That it would mean I wouldn't be able to drive myself back home. As Dr. Tanna explained this to me, I tried to remain calm. Who knew? I had to stay focused and not think about what could go wrong. I was talking to myself a mile a minute, reassuring myself knowing the unexpected was around the corner. They began to prep me for the fillers. I chatted with the PA, trying to keep myself distracted. She explained the process, which was so fascinating. The technology was just amazing. The process began with magnetically matching the port to the entry point underneath the skin, then marking an 'x' where the needle would be inserted, which is attached to the saline bag. Once the needle was in place, Dr. Tanna simply pumped the saline into the tissue expanders. *Wow*, I thought. *Not too bad*. There definitely was a strong sense of pressure, but I didn't find it painful. (Dr. Tanna did warn me that I would need to take some Tylenol when I got home, due to some pain from the skin stretching.) He explained I would have to repeat this procedure every couple of weeks, until I was satisfied with the size. The reason it was spread out over a few weeks, was so that the body could have time to heal in between procedures. This part of the process gave me a strange, bizarre feeling. I suddenly began to feel the expansion, I had breasts again. I imagined the more fill inserted into the tissue expanders, the more bulkiness I would feel. I was pleasantly surprised that I was able to drive myself home. This was a piece of cake. My spirits were up, and I was proud of myself for being brave. I did not allow my fear to stand in the way of my determination. That night Dr. Tanna called to check on me and see how I was handling the pain. "What pain?" I asked. "You mean you have no pain? That's great," he said. "Dr. Tanna, I never took the Tylenol you told me to take. Did you expect me to have pain? Because I'm actually fine!" He was very happy about how I was doing. I did have a high tolerance for pain. I considered myself lucky that I didn't have to depend on pain meds. Going into this journey, I promised myself that I would not abuse my body with medicine, and I kept the promise. Every time I had surgery, the prescriptions would be called into the pharmacy and I would never pick them up. My body had no tolerance for them. I think my doctors thought that I was literally crazy, but I knew this was the way I had to do it. I welcomed this part of my journey with open arms, no fear only positivity.

I had my next few fills throughout the months of January and February. March 9th, 2017, was an exciting day. This was the day I would receive my last fill. The four fills were easier than I had ever expected. I thought this was going to be a happy day because the new "girls" were brimming and almost ready to come out. I could not wait to have them removed in a few weeks. Every time my breast were filled, they became more and more bulky, making it difficult and uncomfortable. They were beginning to sit very high. I used to laugh and say, "I think I can touch my chin to my foobs." I could not wait to get these foobs out of my body. Recognizing I would never have my real breasts again was a struggle and something I had to welcome and accept. I was the type of person who never wanted to be looked at by other women and have them think, "Oh, look at her fake boobs." I was very self-conscious. There wasn't much hiding I could do. These "girls" were getting bigger and bigger. I began to feel very uncomfortable in my own skin. I truly looked ridiculous with these tissue expanders. The more they were filled the higher the breasts got, and the more impossible it was to hide them. I knew it was only temporary, but I hated them. My anxiety level was reaching an all time high. I kept reminding myself that I was almost at the finish line. I began to pack on some weight, which was another thing that made me feel self-conscious. Not only was I suffering from anxiety, I felt a little depressed. My insomnia became so prevalent that I began to have night terrors. I would wake up to terrible nightmares of giant bugs on the wall or hanging from the ceiling. I thought I was losing my mind. I also began to have problems with my blood pressure. I was slowly losing control, thinking to myself quite often, *Did I make a mistake? Was this too much for me to handle? Maybe I wasn't as strong as I thought I was.* It was a combination of anxiety, depression and insomnia that fed the weight gain. I had packed on about 35 pounds. I had never experienced anything like this. My health was spiraling out of control. Not having a spouse or a partner by my side to share my feelings with was also very difficult. There was always one person whom I knew heard me . . . my mom. There was a lot of alone time, and many lonely nights of soul searching. No matter how many friends or family members I had, I didn't have the right person next to me. There was no one to hold me and comfort me. There were plenty of nights when I cried, and woke up wishing I had someone to wrap their arms around me and tell me it was all going to be okay. I was single and my girlfriends were insisting that I should start going on dates. No way, I thought. I was not ready to be in a relationship. Besides, I was feeling insecure about myself. I was extremely uncomfortable with how I looked. I had no self-esteem and I needed time. I wasn't ready to test the waters, not now. The first thing I needed to do before I even thought about dating was to get the tissue expanders out! The truth was this was all so terrifying. I was able to put up a good front. No matter how prepared I thought I was, I never could have known that this path was going to be this strenuous. I did recognize how truly blessed I was to have some of the most amazing doctors, family and friends. They were constantly concerned and checking on me.

Walking in for the last fill was both exciting and nerve-wracking. Dr. Tanna walked in with the physician's assistant, and began to explain that this fill might be different from the others. Handing me Tylenol, even though I'd never taken it before, he explained that I might experience some pain with this last procedure. There would be a lot of skin stretching. Reluctantly, I took Tylenol. I had been fine all along, why should this be any different? I figured I'm good, right? Who knew I would need it. I was certainly naive. They began to add the final fill. Suddenly, I started to feel this enormous pressure and discomfort. I guess Dr. Tanna must have seen my reaction, because he asked me, "Are you okay?" After all I'd been through, I knew I could do this. I kept telling myself to calm down, it was just a little agony. But the reality was that this was a new type of pain that I had never encountered. It was pressure on my chest and I felt like I couldn't breathe. I was in panic mode. I managed to stay strong through the procedure. Dr. Tanna was finally finished. Sitting in the office for a few minutes, I was able to regain my composure and head home. After sitting in the car for a while, I decided it was time to try and drive. As I pulled out of the parking lot, I talked myself into calmness, but the pressure was getting worse and the pain was escalating. I'm sure that my panicked frame of mind was making it appear more chronic than it was. I felt like there was an elephant on my chest and I could not breathe. The pressure got so bad that I had to pull over on the parkway. I immediately called Dr. Tanna. My condition was surprising to him, because I always made things look easy. As I sat in complete panic on the shoulder of the parkway, he had to talk me off the ledge. He explained that what I was feeling was normal, and I had been lucky to not have encountered this with any other fills. That's why he gave me the Tylenol during the procedure. He knew! I hung out on the side of the road for some time. I was able to finally pull it together and drive the rest of the way home. By the time I arrived at my apartment, I was emotionally drained. I was a complete mess, I couldn't function. All I wanted to do was rip out the expanders and sleep this off. As I got comfortable, I began to realize how fortunate I was to not have encountered this with any of the previous fills. Right then and there, I counted my lucky stars. Eventually I fell asleep, only to be woken up by a phone call from the doctor. I thanked him for always being such a great and compassionate man. I told him I was definitely doing better. By this time it was well into the night, and I needed to rest. I would have done anything to be able to jump into bed and lay on my stomach again! I prayed that by the morning things would be easier. I always had faith that better days were ahead. This seemed to be the rule of thumb lately, to put faith *over* fear.

A few more weeks went by. I needed time to heal, before setting the surgery date to remove the tissue expanders and place the implants. It was all very exciting, things were moving right along. I felt I had waited for this day forever. April 20, 2017, I was at Dr. Tanna's to discuss the surgery, which was set for the next day. We discussed silicone vs saline, decided on shape and size, and the fat grafting that was needed to fill in around the implants. I was ecstatic! It was a new lease on life. Finally, the final stages. I couldn't believe we were approaching what seemed to be the tail end of the journey. And so much of this voyage was without hiccups. I knew how blessed I was to have exceptional care, I never took it for granted. So here we were, April 21st. The day I'd been dreaming about a lot lately. My girlfriend was gracious enough to offer me a ride to my surgery again. I knew I couldn't possibly think about doing this alone. Sometimes I had to deflate my own bubble, and step on my pride. I couldn't be that superwoman, or on my own today. The ride there was very upbeat, we cracked jokes about my new foobs. I was glad to have a laugh, realizing that things in life could have been worse. We laughed about how I would have the best boobs in the nursing home. My girlfriend even brought me a little gift of new lip gloss and a mirror. Anything to make me smile. "A girl always needs a new lipstick, right?" she said. I was so grateful for all she had done. When I arrived at the hospital, I was nervous as all hell yet excited. The nurses got me ready for the surgery, quickly and efficiently. This process was so well-rehearsed. It was going to be easy today, compared to the other surgeries I had been through. Dr. Tanna came in to say hi. He explained the incisions and drew where he would be doing the fat grafting. To tell you the truth I was more nervous about the liposuction than anything else! I heard it would require a little bit of a recovery and it would be uncomfortable. Without hesitation I had to put the fear aside and do what was needed. Jumping right in, the surgery went pretty quickly (they all seemed to fly by). I woke up very sore and soon thereafter, I felt the elephant-like pressure on my chest again. I was told I was going to feel this, so I tried to keep myself calm. There was pressure, but not like the last time. The pain was bad but not unbearable. I kept telling myself I had definitely been through worse. I knew what to expect. After spending some time in recovery, I got the okay to head home with strict instructions. My girlfriend helped me get dressed so I could get home to that ever-present recliner. I spent months on this chair, what was another few weeks. It was beginning to get monotonous. I would think to myself, *Will I ever be able to sleep in a bed again?* It was so uncomfortable, but I don't know what I would have done without it. Once I arrived home, I slept the entire day away. I knew that with each day now, I would grow stronger. *Let the healing begin*, I kept saying. I was more anxious than anything else to see my new set of foobs. *Would I like them? Would I hate them? Would I ever embrace them?* Who knew! I did know one thing for sure, there was no returning them. They were mine. I was the new proud owner of these bad boys! There were no refunds or exchanges! Just knowing I had these foreign objects in my body made me uneasy. But I knew all the pros and cons going into this. I lost a part of my body that identified me as a woman, and now I was regaining what was lost. I was anxious about my post-op checkup. It was a little different than the others. I couldn't open the surgical bra to peek. There was no way for me to view them until Dr. Tanna removed the bandages.

The unveiling day was finally here, April 27 2017. I remember waking up with sheer excitement. I could not wait to get to his office. The anticipation was killing me. I wasn't able to drive, so I planned for someone to take me to the appointment. I was scared and beyond excited on the way to the doctor. I kept thinking, *what if I hate them?* I had this pit in my stomach and I could feel my heart racing. Thoughts were spinning like a hamster wheel in my head. My girlfriend was making me laugh and cracking jokes once again about having the best "foobs" when we got older, we needed to find the humor. Arriving at the office, Dr. Tanna walked in and greeted me with a great big smile. "You ready?" he asked. "As ready as I'll ever be," I answered. He opened the surgical bra, and the feeling was so strange. For the first time in months, I felt whole. I watched his face for some sort of reaction. I felt my eyes well up. This was a very emotional moment for me. For the first time in what seemed to be an eternity, I felt like a woman again. I still had a long way to go to fully heal. Dr. Tanna held a mirror to let me look at myself. I was staring, amazed at how realistic they looked. They weren't perfect, but they weren't perfect before either. There were things that needed to be tweaked, but damn I looked good! *This man was an angel with the hands of gold*, I thought. It would definitely take some adjusting, but overall I felt LIKE A WOMAN. I didn't feel like I was missing part of what made me complete. I looked at my girlfriend for her reaction. "Jo, you look amazing," she said. She was blown away by the final result. I couldn't help but give Dr. Tanna a hug. At this moment, he was my hero. I could never thank him enough. Even though I had a lot of healing ahead, I couldn't help but smile! Dr. Tanna then turned to me and asked, "Where do you find your strength? How is it that you're so strong all the time? You drive yourself to most of your own appointments with little to no support. I poke and prod you, and you never cry or flinch. I only see you smiling." I looked at him and felt my eyes well up. Every time I walked through Dr. Tanna's doorway, smiling, it was the polka face I knew I had to wear. Always focusing on keeping a tight hold on the Wonder Woman shield, suddenly I felt emotional. Turning to him I replied, "I don't know, maybe I got it from my loved ones that I lost. I learned at a very young age that when life gets tough you fight hard. I have carried this strength with me since I lost my boyfriend." This was the first time Dr. Tanna had ever seen any vulnerability in me. I was trying hard to hold back the tears. I knew if I blinked they would roll down my cheeks. I looked at him and said jokingly, "Well, I'm about to cry now!" We both laughed. When Dr. Tanna recognized my courage, it affirmed my accomplishment. On this day I walked out with a new sense of confidence. This was the first day of my new life. A life that had escaped breast cancer. A life of not asking, *when will it get me?* A life so different from the path the women in my family had walked. A life that I had chosen for myself. I could breathe easier. It was the life I wished my mother would have chosen for herself. I could feel the sense of pride that my mom felt for me. I knew she and my grandmother were with me every step of the way, shining down on me, acknowledging my role in stopping the horrific cancer from attacking any other woman in our family. This was by far the most emotional day yet. I looked up at the sky and said, "I hope I made you proud Mom."

Once home, all I wanted to do was repeatedly open the surgical bra so I could take a peek. I knew I had to keep them supported, and wear the contraption as much as possible, but it was hopeless, I kept peeking. I dreamt about the day I could actually wear a sports bra again, and sleep in my own bed. With every passing day, I knew I was moving closer to normalcy. This was what kept me going. The worst was over and behind me, I had nothing left to do but heal. I was excited to start living once again. I was finally moving towards a good place. Even though I was still struggling with the weight gain, anxiety and depression, I slowly began to create change. I saw that the road ahead was leading to brighter days, and this made me look at life differently.

The summer was fast approaching. With no revision surgeries in sight until August, I began to exercise again, regained control of my health, and slowly dropped some weight. I was starting to see change I looked for. I was also looking forward to the new year. In March of 2018, I would be celebrating a milestone birthday, I was turning 50! I decided that after all I had been through, and my new found perspective on life I would throw myself a 50th birthday party. I finally had something to look forward to. I was also thrilled and honored that Dr. Tanna called to ask if I would be willing to help with a campaign that he was running for breast cancer. Expressing that he always admired my smile and positivity whenever I came to appointments, he wanted people to hear my story. I was humbled. I knew that women would be looking to me for inspiration and listening to my mother's story of bravery. Throughout my journey, I always tried to remain calm and positive. I always looked to others for inspiration, now it was my turn to reassure and encourage. Of course I said yes to the campaign, I was excited to be a part of something so impactful. This was proof that I persevered. It was a badge of honor that I would wear. I began to see the light, the sunshine peering into the wind tunnel that I was about to exit and leave behind. When in the storm, I adjusted my sails . . . and the storm passed.

Epilogue

March came and went, and my 50th birthday party was a big hit. For the first time in over a year I felt alive again. The journey was not yet complete, I faced another surgery in April 2018, that would consist of a breast revision, with liposuction and fat grafting. Just another mark on the board, at this point. The surgery was a success and all that was needed were follow up visits. Time to heal once again, and seriously focus on my health. I decided to take a serious measure of action to combat the weight I had gained, so I called a health coach friend who had been talking to me about an optimal health and wellness program. Together we decided that this would be a good fit for me, not only as a client but as a coach as well! This was the transformation and accountability I needed to get back to good health. I had to jump in feet first and swim. With the help of a great coach, I was able to drop another 25 pounds. This was exactly what I needed at this time in my life. My confidence was back, and I began to inspire others to do the same. I was also mentoring women for Dr. Tanna at the time. This was a win/win for me. I was helping women get through some of the most difficult of times, and coaching many clients back to better health. This became a rewarding and fulfilling experience. I was teaching women their health mattered and that proper nutrition was important, especially when it came to high risk breast cancer. For the first time in a long time, I felt empowered to influence others towards better health. I had created a trilogy of change for myself. No more depression, no more anxiety, only feelings of happiness. I had been thirsting for this change, on the long, long road traveled. After all these years, I found love in the most incredible man, while at the same time another was swept away. My father, who was my stability, my life teacher, and protector was suddenly gone. I spoke to him at nine in the evening, and by eleven I received the dreaded call. How could I have ever known that would be our last goodbye and I love you?

I continue to strive to create a worry-free life from cancer for others as I did for myself. Teaching to take fear, and making it fight, kicking breast cancer to the curb before it has the chance to get anyone else. I feel accomplished. I took the stance, I fought the fight. I have evolved into a new person-a person who embraces growth. I am now an individual who knows how to heal, and create memories through new life experiences. While writing this book, I have taken what I learned to unleash the pain that I harbored for so long, and instead respect and accept my mother's decision. I consistently remind myself of the bravery and courage that my beautiful grandmother, mother, and aunts always displayed. And I have learned that with determination we can be the authors of our own story. Never be afraid to write your own. Remember to always put **faith** *over fear!*

Acknowledgments

There are so many people that I owe thanks to when writing this dedication. First and foremost, my children who stand at the forefront of my life. My driving forces, Rocco and Christian. You are the ones that light the flame within me everyday. You inspire me to recognize my worth and to reach the unreachable. I thank you both for all of your unconditional love and support, and most of all for being the most amazing men in my life. You make me proud to be your mother and I love you both endlessly.

Secondly, I'd like to give my deepest appreciation and thanks to two of the most compassionate, caring, kind and empathetic doctors . . . Dr. Alan Kadison, and Dr. Neil Tanna. When I say "thank you" from the bottom of my heart, I truly mean it. I am grateful and blessed that I had you to navigate me through this journey of uncertainty that I was so hesitant to walk. Dr. Kadison, you are the epitome of all that a doctor should be. From day one, you reassured me of all my doubts. You confirmed to me that I was making the right decision, by helping me understand the importance of my genetics. I thank you Dr. Kadison for fighting the fight and never giving up on me. Dr. Tanna, from the day I met you I knew I was in safe hands. Your confidence swiftly became my confidence. Easing my worries and fears, you taught me to take this day by day, and not dwell on what was ahead. I have new found strength and character thanks to you. Thank you for making me feel whole again. Dr. Kadison and Dr.

Tanna, you both have a gift in what I refer to as "hands of gold." Any woman should feel honored to call either one of you their doctors. I will be forever grateful that I met you.

To my friends and family, especially the ones who encouraged me to write this memoir. I can say I had some pretty amazing people in my life along this crazy ride. The first acknowledgement goes to the most impactful person in my life, who is unfortunately no longer with me . . . my dad. Daddy, I could have never made it through this journey without you and your continued love and support. You always knew the right thing to say or do. Even when you had no words, you held my hand tight, and I knew it was all going to be okay. I love you forever. To all the girls, the ones who made me laugh, or made me cry from your encouraging words . . . I love you all! Whether it be a beautiful card, or a simple gift you sent, I am forever grateful. Thank you! To my beautiful friend Vicki: Thank you for your continuous support, the endless lifts to appointments, the belly laughs (when I thought I'd pop a stitch due to you hitting every pothole imaginable). Or a simple pretty new lipstick to brighten my day. I love you to the moon and back. To my soul sister Lucienne. Thank you for your constant words of encouragement throughout this journey. For always reminding me of my worth, and for never letting me dream alone . . . I love you fiercely! Thank you to my sister-in-law Yvette for the endless hours of editing. And my girlfriends who have read these chapters endlessly with me, always giving me the constructive criticism and advice that was needed. I love you all! To Savannah and Kayla, I love you both and thank you for loving my boys the way you do. Thank you for being a part of my life, you're both very special to me. To my second mom, Nurse Fran. Thank you for always being the voice of calm and a book of knowledge. But most of all for holding me up on that most dreadful day when my knees went weak. I speak for my mom when I say, we love you! To my two warrior aunts. I love and admire you both, and will always see you as the most courageous and brave women. Gioia, I am honored that you have allowed me into your sacred world, sharing your most intimate stories, and for writing the forward. You give new meaning to the word "rock star." Love you girl! To my family, especially my brothers, my cousin who is a brother to me, and my cousin . . . my crib sister, thank you for supporting my decision from day one. You were the ones who saw the fear in me, you were the ones who shared the commonality of pain when we lost our beautiful mother. Thank you for lifting me up when I felt like I was falling. I love you all. To my love, who walked into my life at the tail end of this journey as if you didn't skip a beat. I now know that God had a plan. Thank you for allowing me to trust in you, and for always being an empathetic man. Most importantly, for holding my hand as I was tiring to cross the finish line, reminding me that I wasn't alone. Thank you for all your love and support in writing this book. Tiamo!

Last but certainly not least. The true inspiration and dedication is to my Mother and my Grandmother. You were by far the two most courageous and beautiful women in my life. I'm handing the world this book to read the legacy of two brave women. Women who have molded me into the person that I am today. I admire you both tremendously, and I will never give up this fight. I will continue to bring awareness until we see the changes that are so desperately needed. I know that from above, you will both be by my side guiding me, every step of the way. I love you forever!